The Messianic Mo

A Field Gui
Evangelical Christians

from Jews for Jesus

The Messianic Movement:
A Field Guide for Evangelical Christians
from Jews for Jesus

Rich Robinson, General Editor

Naomi Rose Rothstein, Contributing Editor

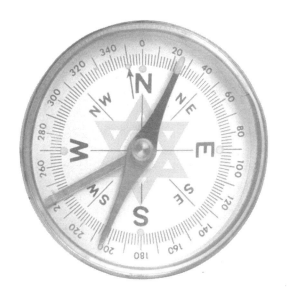

Purple Pomegranate Productions
A division of Jews for Jesus

The Messianic Movement: A Field Guide for Evangelical Christians
from Jews for Jesus
Rich Robinson, General Editor
Naomi Rose Rothstein, Contributing Editor
© Copyright 2005 by Purple Pomegranate Productions
(a division of Jews for Jesus®)
Cover design and layout by David Yapp

For more information, including reprint permission, write to:
Jews for Jesus®
60 Haight Street
San Francisco, CA 94102
USA
www.jewsforjesus.org

ISBN 10: 1-881022-62-5
ISBN 13: 978-1-881022-62-6

Introduction

What is the "Messianic movement" and what's the point of a "field guide" to it?

Hardly a day goes by that the Jews for Jesus office doesn't get calls from people asking questions pertaining to the Messianic movement. We thought that it would be helpful to put together some material that would answer many of those questions.

Though the existence of Messianic Jews dates back to the early Church—when Jewish believers in Jesus retained their distinctive Jewish lifestyle for several centuries—the specific term "Messianic" experienced a surge in popularity in the 1970s when it was used to describe a moving of Jewish people to faith in Y'shua (Jesus) in the context of Jewish culture. While the term "Messianic" was never formally defined, it was broadly used to describe someone who was both Jewish and a believer in Jesus.

Today the term "Messianic" has been adopted—and sometimes co-opted—by numerous groups and theologies. And so we constantly receive inquiries from Christians, both Jewish and Gentile, who want to know about a particular Messianic congregation, or a certain "Hebrew roots of the Christian faith" teacher, or a person who says the Church is the lost tribe of Ephraim, or someone who advocates for something called "Nazarene Judaism." It seems that when a group or congregation or teaching institution puts "Jesus" and "Jewish" together in its name or philosophy, it is seen as part of the Messianic movement.

It is because of this ambiguity that we wrote this book, which we hope will serve as a "field guide" to the Messianic Jewish movement. Given today's diverse usage of the term "Messianic," it should be clear that there is no founder or single spokesperson for the terms "Messianic," "Messianic movement," "Messianic Jew" or "Messianic Judaism." While we might prefer to restrict the term "Messianic movement" to simply mean Jews who follow Jesus, this is not possible. We will take an inclusive look at various trends and organizations that some might call "Messianic"—from the healthy to the unhealthy, from the kosher and to the not-so-kosher. Our aim is to cover not only Jews who believe in Jesus and keep Jewish customs and practices, but also any Christian group who claims to be exploring the Jewishness of the Christian faith. We also wanted to include anyone else who purports to live according to the teachings and practices of the first followers of Jesus—whether or not they accept His deity.

"Part One: The Movement" surveys the various organizations under the "Messianic" umbrella: (1) Jewish missions; (2) Messianic congregations; (3) voluntary associations; (4) umbrella organizations; (5) educational institutions; (6) philo-Semitic or "love Israel" organizations. Each chapter includes an introduction, background and analysis of the current scene. These are also followed by suggestions for further reading. Please note that all web URLs were last accessed on July 1, 2005, and some may no longer be active. For your convenience, we have listed all the URLs cited in one place at: http://www.jewsforjesus.org/publications/fieldguide

"Part Two: Movements Within the Movement" surveys some general trends that cut across many Messianic organizations. First, we look at the essential Jewishness of Christianity, especially as regards the main doctrines of the faith. Then there is a brief overview of the place of the Law in the life of

Jewish believers and, thirdly, a look at the "Torah-observant" aspects of the Messianic movement. Finally, we include an essay on the continued need for direct Jewish evangelism. And we've included some (what we hope are) helpful appendices.

This book seeks to help people think discerningly about those things that have to do with Jesus and Jews. While lines are drawn around aspects of the movement that are sub-biblical or run contrary to accepted Christian teaching, at the same time we wish to affirm the healthy diversity that comprises the movement of Jewish believers in Jesus. Any survey of this kind will end up naming particular organizations and individuals, for the various groups mentioned have for the most part promulgated their ideas publicly, thereby inviting public response. Yet, we want to emphasize that we uphold or take issue with perspectives, not people. At the time this guide was compiled, the statements herein adequately reflected the positions of the people and organizations they are attributed to. Yet we'd like to point out that we realize that people's opinions and positions are subject to change. Should a statement or position we've published no longer be the view of a group or individual cited, we would welcome hearing about it for future editions of the *Field Guide*. We also recognize that we have not included every possible group. Should you have questions not covered in this field guide, we will do our best to suggest where you might look for answers.

Our hope is to challenge followers of Jesus, whether Jewish or Gentile, to follow Paul's exhortation: "...whatever things are true, whatever things are noble, whatever things are just, whatever things are pure, whatever things are lovely, whatever things are of good report, if there is any virtue and if there is anything praiseworthy—meditate on these things" (Philippians 4:8).

—Rich Robinson

Contents

Part One

The Movement

Chapter One
Jewish Missions

INTRODUCTION

Mission agencies frequently focus on reaching specific people groups, whether geographic (missions to one region), ethnic (missions to particular tribal peoples) or socio-economic (missions to students or professionals of some kind). Likewise, there are missions particularly directed to proclaiming the gospel to the Jewish people; their missionaries are sent by and work alongside local church congregations to that purpose. Jewish missions have been affiliated with various evangelical denominations and doctrinal positions. By undertaking financial and prayer support, churches and individual Christians act as senders of the missionaries. In this, Jewish missions follow the *modus operandi* of Protestant mission agencies everywhere.

If you see someone distributing Jewish-oriented tracts in public places, or view an ad in a newspaper or magazine proclaiming that Jesus is the Jewish Messiah, or hear someone preaching a gospel sermon at a venue that Jewish people attend, or know of a Bible study group for Jewish seekers, then you have seen a Jewish mission in action. The primary tasks of Jewish mission agencies are gospel proclamation, follow-up and discipleship.

There are some aspects of Jewish missions that make the work uniquely challenging. The first challenge is geographical: Jewish people are scattered throughout the globe. The second challenge is sociological: Jewish people come from a vast array of backgrounds and belief systems, ranging from atheists to ultra-Orthodox, and everything in between. In fact, there is such a variety of worldviews

represented among this one people group that there is a
saying that goes, "If you ask two Jews a question, you'll get
three opinions." These challenges have been present since
the beginning of Jewish missions and explain in part why
there have never been massive numbers of Jewish people
coming to faith in Christ at one time.

JEWISH MISSIONS: A HISTORIC OVERVIEW

We know from the Book of Acts that the early Jewish believers
in Jesus were missionaries—first to the lost sheep of the
house of Israel, and later to the other nations, or Gentiles. In
those days the question was not, "How can someone be a Jew
for Jesus?" but rather, "How can a Gentile be for Jesus without
first becoming a Jew?"

Before too long the Church became predominantly Gentile.
While a remnant of Jewish believers remained, by and large
the Jewish people were badly in need of others to extend
the love of Christ to them, as the early Jewish believers did
for Gentiles. Yet the concept of Jewish evangelism and
Jewish missions is relatively new and is still considered
somewhat controversial.

It wasn't until the 1800s that we saw the formal institution of
Jewish missions. Previously, there were groups like the
Moravians who felt that they should be telling Jews about
Jesus. But outside of the endeavors of a few individuals, there
was little organized effort to bring the message of the Messiah
to the Jewish people.

Perhaps the issue was avoided for so many centuries because of
the patristic antipathy toward the Jews. When we read the tirades
of some of the early church fathers against the Jewish people, we
should not wonder that the Church adopted a prejudiced
viewpoint and viewed Jewish culture and religion negatively.[1]

There was an increase in Jewish missions activity from about 1880, at a time when anti-Semitic persecution was rising in the Russian Empire, and when Jewish immigration, especially to the United States, was reaching unprecedented levels. In order to encourage compassion for Jewish people, mission publications appealed to Christian contributors by depicting the pitiable poverty in which many Jewish people in Eastern Europe found themselves.

In Europe, missions to the Jews were founded in several countries, particularly Great Britain, Norway and Finland. The British missions sent out workers throughout Europe and overseas. The Norwegian and Finnish missions gave particular attention to the increasing number of Jews who were returning to the land of Israel. As their work in Israel developed, there was a growing desire to form indigenous Hebrew-speaking congregations in the Land.

By the early decades of the 20th century, a number of well-organized missionary societies had arisen in the USA as well: the American Board of Missions to the Jews (ABMJ, earlier known as the Williamsburg Mission to the Jews); the Presbyterian Mission to the Jews; the Chicago Hebrew Mission; the American Association for Jewish Evangelism (a 1940s breakaway from the ABMJ).

The difficulty in integrating new Jewish believers in Jesus from Eastern European cultures into largely Anglo-Saxon Christian congregations led some to favor the establishment of Hebrew Christian congregations. The Presbyterian Mission to the Jews led the way, establishing Jewish congregations in several U.S. cities: Chicago; New York; Los Angeles; Philadelphia; Baltimore.

Jewish missions have reflected a variety of Christian traditions. There have been Lutheran Jewish missions, Presbyterian Jewish missions, Christian Reformed Jewish missions, Baptist Jewish missions, Assembly of God Jewish missions and Anglican/Episcopal efforts, as well as independent missions. Among denominationally based Jewish missions, some were particularly active prior to the Second World War.

With the rise of Nazism, certain missionaries to European Jews moved to Great Britain and the United States. Some of these missionaries were apologists whose work still influences Jewish missions today.[2]

Hundreds of thousands of Jews came out of the Holocaust and arrived in the United Kingdom, America and Israel with absolutely nothing. Medical clinics were opened to care for the Jewish poor. Eventually, the governments in these countries began to assist in such relief efforts and by the middle of the century there was no longer a real need for the clinics.

Following the Holocaust, various denominations largely curtailed or ended their Jewish missions programs. Some adopted a "two-covenant" theology, which says that Jewish people have no need of the gospel, since God already made a covenant with them through Abraham (see "Further Reading" below). Even evangelicals increasingly came under the sway of this sort of thinking and embraced dialogue or friendship with the Jewish community as a substitute for proclamation. In the past few decades, however, the Lutheran Church-Missouri Synod has strongly reaffirmed the need for Jewish evangelism and has established a growing Jewish mission work, and the Southern Baptists, amidst much media coverage, have publicly endorsed Jewish evangelism. Some work also is carried on by the Christian & Missionary Alliance (C&MA), the Presbyterian Church in America (PCA) and the Assemblies of God (AOG). Alongside denominational efforts, independent Jewish missions continue, though consolidated to a handful of international

missions, such as Jews for Jesus, founded in 1973, Chosen People
Ministries, Christian Jew Foundation Ministries, Ariel Ministries,
AMF International, Friends of Israel, Christian Witness to Israel
(CWI) and The Church's Ministry Among Jewish People (CMJ).
Several local missions are currently active, including Light of
Messiah Ministries in Atlanta, Georgia; Christians Announcing
Israel's Messiah in Philadelphia, Pennsylvania; and Messianic
Good News in Wading River, New York.

JEWISH MISSIONS METHODS
Jewish mission agencies encompass a wide variety of
approaches. Few Jewish people will seek out information
about Jesus on their own, so a certain amount of creativity
and persistence is necessary. Most mission organizations
have employed one or more of the following methods.

Literature and Media Development and Distribution
Evangelistic literature development and distribution have long
played a vital role in Jewish missions. Because Jewish people
are located throughout the world, it's important to have Bibles
and other literature, including articles, pamphlets and tracts,
available in several languages. It's also crucial that these
materials be carefully constructed with Jewish sensitivities in
mind. Over the years, tracts (sometimes called "broadsides")
have become shorter and more humorous to accommodate a
more "fast food, fast everything" generation. Tracts often
contain testimonies of Jewish believers and Scripture verses.

Multimedia efforts such as videos, DVDs and CD-ROMs are
being used more effectively. Often such programs feature
moving testimonies, apologetics information, answers to
frequently asked questions or even interactive games.

As for the challenge of getting these resources into the hands
of Jewish seekers, tracts are often distributed in mass numbers

in public places where Jewish people live and work. Jewish-seeker-friendly publications (or evangelistic book or media offers) are also directly mailed to Jewish homes. Sometimes mission groups set up resource tables at events such as fairs or festivals or on college campuses, or a mission might conduct public screenings of multimedia presentations.

Messianic Music

Messianic music, in addition to its value as a valid expression of worship, has proved to be a good evangelistic tool. Jewish seekers are invited to evangelistic music concerts in secular halls, on college campuses and in churches. Sometimes Messianic music groups obtain a permit to perform in a public square or park, which almost always gathers a crowd of people and provides an opportunity to share the gospel in a creative way.

Radio and Television Ministries

Radio and television outreach continues to grow. Some of the more widely known television programs are "Zola Levitt Presents," "Jewish Voice Today" with Jonathan Bernis, "Sid Roth's Messianic Vision," and "Jewish Jewels" with Neil and Jamie Lash. These shows, which focus on educating Christians about Jews and Jewish evangelism, often reach interested Jewish people who happen to listen in. The increasing popularity of radio via the Internet has enabled radio efforts such as Messianic Bureau International's "Messianic Jewish Radio" and "Messianic Minutes." Programs typically feature testimonies of Jewish believers in Jesus, Messianic music and Bible teaching.

Cyber-evangelism

Perhaps the newest method of all is electronic evangelism. Just about every middle-class and upwardly mobile home in the western world owns or has access to a computer. Several ministries have developed and are effectively using websites and chat rooms to proclaim Y'shua.

Secular Media Campaigns

Another newer method of evangelism that has been significantly employed since the early 1980s is the publication of gospel statements in secular media, including newspapers and magazines with a large Jewish readership. Gospel statements directed to Jewish people are also found on billboards, as well as on secular radio and TV. At the beginning of this new generation of missionaries, most of the protest against the gospel stemmed from one statement: "Jews don't believe in Jesus." Now the fact that Jews do believe in Jesus is out in the open, thanks in large part to use of the secular media.

Children's Work

Evangelism to Jewish children often occurs in the context of ministry to Jewish believing children at summer camps, retreats and Bible clubs. Parents must, of course, give permission for their children to participate in these activities.

Holiday Outreaches

Jewish mission agencies and Messianic congregations conduct outreaches during the Jewish High Holy days. Constituents and congregational members are encouraged to bring Jewish friends and family to Rosh Hashanah (New Year) and Yom Kippur (Day of Atonement) services, in addition to public Passover seders. These are often worship services with evangelistic emphases. Some local ministries have developed creative initiatives for Jewish community outreach, such as hand delivering holiday gift baskets to Jewish friends.

Personal Visits

The heart of missions work is sitting down one-on-one with Jewish people who have been contacted through one of the

above methods and studying Jesus' claims with them.
Sometimes these connections are initially made on the street,
from calling Jewish people from a prepared phone list or from
making a door-to-door inquiry. Sometimes Jewish people
respond to an ad or program they saw or heard. Whatever the
case, it is this personal connection that remains the primary
goal of Jewish missions.

To read more specific information about current initiatives in
Jewish missions, we refer you to "Jewish Evangelism: A Call to
the Church" (see "Further Reading" below).

PHILOSOPHICAL ISSUES

Like all missionary enterprises, Jewish missions have had to
wrestle with issues of indigenous culture and contextualization of
the gospel. Nineteenth-century missionaries often superimposed
the culture of the sponsoring country onto the gospel message.
In the second half of the twentieth century, recognition of the
interplay between gospel and culture has allowed for indigenous
gospel proclamation and expression. This recognition has
become an integral part of the way most Jewish missions work.

There has always been a tension in Jewish missions: How
could a Jewish believer in Jesus be an integral part of the
entire Body of Christ and yet still express his or her faith in an
"indigenous" way? Typical solutions were for missions to
encourage fellowships of Jewish believers in Jesus in addition
to attendance at churches, or to sponsor Jewish holiday
events. In effect, the missions acted as a special-interest group
to Jewish believers in the same way that a campus Christian
ministry acts as a special-interest group to students, who
attend its functions as well as their own churches.

Another solution was the creation of "Hebrew-Christian
churches," the forerunners of modern Messianic

congregations. The "Hebrew-Christian churches" were sometimes independent affairs or were sometimes sponsored under the auspices of a church denomination. But the Hebrew-Christian churches sparked a lively debate of their own over whether Jewish believers should have their own separate congregations (see chapter 1.2).

Certain Jewish missions continue to plant Messianic congregations as a method for evangelism today. Some in the Messianic movement have further suggested that evangelism best takes place through Messianic congregations and have come to question the necessity for other traditional methods of proclamation.

While evangelism certainly occurs through congregations, it cannot be said that the Messianic congregational movement has seen more fruitfulness than missions. One writer states that 98% of the Jewish members of Messianic congregations came to faith in Jesus through the witness of a Gentile Christian.[3] Additionally, a significant number of Messianic congregational leaders came to faith through Jewish mission agencies.

Missions and congregations do not need to be mutually exclusive approaches; they have worked in tandem in the past and continue to do so today.

CONCLUSION

The major Jewish missions dedicated to proclamation evangelism retain close connections with the Church and remain firmly evangelical in theology. The materials, methodology and models for Jewish missions adapt according to the times, but overall, the mindset of the Jewish community has not changed, nor has our message of salvation. The mentality of those who would evangelize the Jewish people continues to be based on the mind of Christ.

The motivation to present the gospel to the Jewish people comes from faith-filled people who are propelled by the Holy Spirit and the Word of God. Moreover, Christ Jesus, whether we call Him Y'shua HaMashiach or any other of His legitimate names, will never change. He is our mandate, our motivator and our model from whom we draw our inspiration and support.

FURTHER READING

For your convenience, we have listed all the URLs in this book in one place at: http://www.jewsforjesus.org/publications/ fieldguide

Rosen, Moishe. "Jewish Evangelism, Then and Now," *Jews for Jesus Newsletter*, July 1998. Available online at: http://www.jewsforjesus.org/publications/newsletter/1998_07/th enandnow_pt1

Mishkan: A Theological Forum on Jewish Evangelism 11 (1989), available at online at http://www.caspari.com/mishkan. Issue 11 is given over entirely to a discussion of "two-covenant" theology.

Mishkan 37 (2002), devoted to "19th & 20th Century Contributors to the Messianic Movement" available as a PDF at: http://www.caspari.com/mishkan/zips/mishkan37.pdf

The Digital Jewish Missions History Project, available at: www.lcje.net/history

Tucker, Ruth. *Not Ashamed: The Story of Jews for Jesus*, Multnomah Publishers, 1999.

"A Brief List of Famous Messianic Jews" at: http://www.israelinprophecy.org/live_site/english/brief_list-most_famous_messianic_jews.html

Zaretsky, Tuvya, ed. "Jewish Evangelism: A Call to the
Church." Occasional Paper No. 60, Lausanne Committee for
World Evangelization, 2005. Available at:
http://community.gospelcom.net/lcwe/assets/LOP60_IG31.pdf

Taber, Wes. "Current Trends in Cross-Cultural
Contextualization," paper presented at Lausanne Consultation
on Jewish Evangelism CEO Conference, Dijon, France, May
2005, available at:
http://files.jewsforjesus.org/pdf/other/taber.pdf

See Appendix E for "A Rationale for Jewish Evangelism."

See Appendix F for "The Willowbank Declaration on the
Christian Gospel and the Jewish People."

Notes

1. John Chrysostom, Origen of Alexandria and Martin Luther are
examples of church leaders who made statements about the Jewish
culture and religion that could easily be read as anti-Semitic. See
Hay, Malcolm. "Roots of Christian anti-Semitism," Anti-Defamation
League of B'nai B'rith, 1984.
2. The missionary ranks of the previous generations included
scholars of Hebrew and Scripture. Two of the many who deserve
mention are A.J. Kligerman and his son-in-law, Arthur Kac. They
contributed numerous scholarly articles and books. Many
Christians know the name Jacob Jocz, but comparatively few
know of his brother, Paul Yates. Paul Yates was a student of
rabbinics and Scripture, but most of all he was a superb general
missionary in the San Francisco Bay Area for some 40 years. Then
there were Morris Zutrau, Moses Gitlin and dozens, if not
hundreds, of others who could be mentioned. The last in that line
of rabbinical scholars who were effective for the gospel was
Rachmiel Frydland. He was a brilliant *yeshiva* (school of Jewish

education) student who came to faith just before the Germans marched into Poland. These European-born Jewish apologists argued effectively from Scripture, as well as from Jewish sources such as the Talmud and Responsa (the body of written decisions and rulings given to questions addressed) to make the case for Jesus. Others were not *yeshiva*-trained but still embodied Jewish spirit, such as Fred Kendal and Immanuel Gittell. The archetype of the scholar/missionary would be David Bronstein, Sr., of Chicago. He conducted two divergent missions and pastored what would today be seen as a Messianic congregation.

3. Wasserman, Jeffrey S., *Messianic Jewish Congregations: Who Sold This Business to the Gentiles?* Lanham, MD: University Press of America, 2000, p. 106.

Chapter Two
Messianic Congregations

INTRODUCTION

Messianic congregations are local expressions of the Body of Christ that seek to structure their service and worship along traditional Jewish lines while maintaining that Jesus is the promised Messiah. They are a large, visible part of the modern Messianic movement.

Messianic congregations can be found all around the world both in large cities and small towns, and attract Jewish and non-Jewish believers. The worship structure can vary considerably; many meet on the Jewish sabbath (Friday night or Saturday morning) while some conduct Sunday worship. Most observe the Jewish holidays, looking to Jesus as the fulfillment. In some, worshippers wear *kippot* (skullcaps) or *tallesim* (prayer shawls). In some, the music style is noticeably Jewish with a contemporary flavor; in others traditional Jewish liturgical elements are interwoven. Some congregations have auxiliary organizations such as a sisterhood, a day school or *yeshiva* (Jewish school of learning) modeled on structures similar to those in the mainstream Jewish community.

A BRIEF HISTORY OF MESSIANIC CONGREGATIONS

In the 1880s Joseph Rabinowitz formed a group in Kishinev, Moldavia, called the "Israelites of the New Covenant," which may well be the first modern "Messianic congregation." [1] Prior to the late 19th century, Jewish followers of Jesus worshiped almost exclusively in the local Lutheran or Presbyterian or Anglican churches, as in many cases it was these denominations that sponsored Jewish missions. But the late 19th century brought the rise of Zionism and the awakening of Jewish national consciousness, and it was in that context that Rabinowitz said that Jewish believers could (in fact, should) worship in a way that reflected and affirmed their Jewishness, to show the world that Jews do not cease being Jewish because they believe in Jesus, and in fact, that Jesus was one of "us."

At the same time in North America, the advent of modern Jewish missions prompted some to wonder if it would be helpful to the cause of Jewish evangelism for Jewish believers to form their own congregations that would utilize traditional Jewish forms of worship. Also, Jewish believers faced two problems: (1) they were often not welcome within the church (a situation many Christians today might have trouble picturing), and (2) they were unwelcome in the synagogue.[2]

Still, not everyone was in favor of "Hebrew-Christian churches." In 1915 the newly formed Hebrew-Christian Alliance of America (see chapter 1.3) had a lively debate over the advisability of Jewish believers forming separate congregations—or for that matter, observing any traditional Jewish practices.

However, the ideological/theological questions seemed to take a back seat to pragmatism. So Jewish missions and independent missionaries to the Jewish people in North America sometimes established "Hebrew-Christian churches," such as Jacob Freshman's Hebrew-Christian Church in New York City in the 1880s. In later years there were, among others, The Congregations of the Messiah Within Israel of Los Angeles (formed in 1955); as well as the First Hebrew Christian Church of Chicago (1934); the First Hebrew Christian Church of Philadelphia (1954); and Emmanuel Presbyterian Hebrew Christian Congregation in Baltimore (1963)—all three begun by the Presbyterian church.[3] The fact that a mainline Christian denomination began these congregations tells us that this was not a splinter move made in opposition to the Church, but done out of positive motives—to see Jews remain as Jews within the Body of Christ.[4]

In the 1970s, congregations began to prefer the term "Messianic congregation" to "Hebrew-Christian church," just as many Jewish believers in Jesus gradually began to prefer the term "Messianic Jew" to "Hebrew-Christian."[5] This change was mostly a reflection of trends in the larger Jewish community. In the late 19th and early 20th centuries there arose a sense of "national" Jewish consciousness, and the Jewish community adopted the designation "Hebrew" to express this nationality.[6] Then the rise of the State of Israel and its near-legendary victory in the 1967 war fostered a renewed sense of collective Jewish pride among many American Jews, including Jewish believers.[7] Calling oneself a "Messianic Jew" rather than a "Hebrew-Christian" was a more deliberate way of affirming one's Jewish identity.

At the same time, more Christians began to affirm Jewish believers' choice to retain their identity as Jews. After all, modern missions looked favorably on ethnic churches; there were Korean churches, Chinese churches—why not Jewish ones as well?[8]

However, not all Jewish believers flocked to Messianic congregations. In fact, most continued to attend mainstream churches, but expressed their Jewishness by joining other Jewish believers in fellowship groups that were often sponsored by local Jewish missions. Since many of those Jewish people who came to faith in the early 70s were young and had experienced tensions at home because of their faith, most looked to meet other Jews who believed, whether in Messianic congregations or fellowship groups.

MESSIANIC CONGREGATIONS TODAY

Though there are umbrella organizations for Messianic congregations, not all congregations belong to them; some are independent. Because there is no central organization or registry for all Messianic congregations, it's hard to state exactly how many there are. Jeffrey Wasserman, publishing in the year 2000, suggested that there were 200-250 congregations in North America. Some have been planted by Jewish missions or by Christian denominations. They vary widely in numbers, worship styles, training of leadership and ethnic make-up.

Some Messianic congregations in cities with larger Jewish populations have a solid, traceable history that goes back decades. Beth Yeshua in Philadelphia, Aron Kodesh in Fort Lauderdale, and Beth Israel Worship Center in New Jersey are three of the largest. Some of the other large congregations that reflect the migration of the Jewish population in the U.S. are Baruch Hashem in Dallas, Beth Hallel in Atlanta, Kehilat Ariel in San Diego, and Roeh Israel in Denver. When we say "large" keep in mind that attendance in Messianic congregations can usually be measured at most in the hundreds. On the flipside, most Messianic congregations are much smaller, with an average attendance of 100 or fewer. Some messianic congregations have only a handful of attendees.

It must be noted that most Jewish believers still attend churches, rather than Messianic congregations. Estimates as to the number of Jewish believers in Jesus in the U.S. have varied from a low of 30,000[9] to a high of 600,000 (for all of North America).[10] If one allows for 300[11] Messianic congregations in the U.S. of 60 people each, half of whom are Jewish,[12] then there would be 9,000 Jewish believers in Messianic congregations. Even with the lowest estimate, this

leaves the majority in some other context than that of
Messianic congregations.

What then is happening in the Messianic congregations? Some
missiologists have rejoiced over the Messianic congregational
movement, viewing it as evidence of growth in the number of
Jewish followers of Jesus. But a closer look reveals that few if
any Messianic congregations outside Israel are made up
exclusively of Jews. Most congregations that call themselves
"Messianic" are a mix of Jews and Gentiles, usually
predominantly and sometimes exclusively non-Jewish in
makeup. Many have non-Jewish leadership.[13]

What, then, is the difference between a Messianic
congregation and a church? Some key elements of the
Messianic congregational service might include Hebrew
liturgy, such as reading/chanting from the Torah. Like a
regular synagogue, Messianic congregations often have a
"Torah service" wherein specific portions of the Torah (the
Pentateuch) and Haftorah (the Prophetic Writings) are read in
Hebrew. Sometimes there is a Torah "processional," wherein
the Torah scroll is paraded around the congregation so people
can touch it themselves.

Other Hebrew liturgical aspects of a Messianic congregation
service may include the recitation of the Amidah (the Standing
Prayer) which is comprised of 19 benedictions and is central
to all synagogue services, the Sh'ma in Hebrew and English
("Hear O Israel, the Lord Your God is One God"); this is taken
from Deuteronomy 6:4. Also, at the end of the service, the
Aaronic Benediction may be chanted; this is taken from
Numbers 6:24-26.

The worship at a Messianic congregation will most likely
incorporate Messianic or Jewish gospel praise songs, with

Hebrew and English lyrics interwoven with Israeli folk beats, minor chords and traditional Jewish instruments, such as the dunbek, a middle eastern drum. Some Messianic congregations incorporate what is known as Messianic or "Davidic" worship dance in their services, either performed at the platform or with congregational participation.

Just as there are differences among synagogues in the mainstream Jewish community, so Messianic congregations differ in terms of how much liturgy is used, how much Hebrew is recited and how long the worship and message times are. Some reflect more structured Orthodox Jewish forms and some are more contemporary and free form, like in the Reform Jewish tradition (for more about the different streams of Judaism, please see appendix D). Often the leader of a Messianic congregation will refer to himself or herself as "rabbi"; sometimes not.

The terminology used at Messianic congregations also varies from congregation to congregation, but by and large, a visitor to a Messianic congregation will note that the pulpit is referred to as the *bima*, congregants may use some sort of *siddur*, or liturgy guide to the service, and Jesus is most often referred to as *Y'shua Hamashiach* (Jesus the Messiah) rather than as Jesus. There is usually a lack of overtly Christian symbols, such as crosses, as most congregations want to be sensitive to Jewish people who might be uncomfortable with such symbols. This is easier for some groups than others, since very few Messianic congregations own their own buildings and many share facilities with a local church. Often, the Messianic congregants cover over some of the more overt Christian accoutrements. Instead they might display a Star of David or other Jewish motifs, such as a menorah.

Whether mainstream Jews or new Jewish believers find Messianic congregations to be more comfortable than churches is really a subjective matter. There are Jewish people who have come to faith in Jesus who either weren't raised with much Jewish tradition or were "turned off" to synagogue-style services before they believed in Jesus, and so they often feel less comfortable with all the Jewish elements than one might expect. The same goes for Jewish visitors who don't believe in Jesus. In the U.S., the Jewish parts of the Messianic congregation service might put off secular Jews, and those from more religious backgrounds might feel that the Jewish aspects of the Messianic congregations aren't very authentic. When Lauren Winner, who came to Christianity from more Orthodox surroundings, first visited a Messianic congregation, she expressed her thoughts this way:

> This is how I feel all morning: that Brit Hadashah's Judaism is just raisins added to cake—you notice them, but they don't really change the cake. The structure of the service bears no relation to the Jewish liturgy, and I can't tell if my fellow worshippers think that being Jewish leads them to understand Jesus any differently from Presbyterians down the street. Add Hebrew and Stir.[14]

However, some Jews are drawn to Messianic congregations. Jews for Jesus missionary Chad Elliott claims he "found Jesus in the yellow pages"; while looking for a traditional synagogue to attend, he found one in the phone book that turned out to be a Messianic congregation! Chad kept attending and eventually came to faith in Jesus.

Messianic congregations aren't just a North American phenomenon. They exist in Europe, Russia, even in Africa. And of course, there are several Messianic congregations in Israel. The congregational movement is far from a passing trend. Though some may be fledgling and many contain more Gentiles than Jews, Messianic congregations are likely to continue for some time.

PHILOSOPHICAL ISSUES

In the early days of debating whether there should be "Hebrew-Christian churches," some feared that Jewish believers would isolate themselves from the rest of the Body and raise the "wall of partition" by emphasizing their Jewish distinctiveness. This ongoing debate centers around two questions: (1) Is it right for Jewish believers to separate themselves from the rest of the Body of Christ in this way?; and (2) Is it right for followers of Jesus to observe Old Testament or rabbinic customs and ceremonies?

The question of distinctive ethnic congregations is relevant not only to Jewish believers in Jesus; it has been an ongoing missiological question. Missiologists and church planters speak of the "homogeneous unit principle," whereby separate ethnic congregations are planted—Korean, Chinese, Native American, etc. One reason that is advanced for the validity of this approach is the claim that it leads to an increase in church growth. Others, however, think it is more biblical to form multi-ethnic congregations where the diversity in the Body of Christ is represented—since Christ has broken down the dividing wall between Jews and Gentiles and by implication, all ethnic groups.[15]

In Jewish ministry, the question also raises direct theological concerns, because unlike other ethnic groups, the Scriptures specifically say that the wall of partition *between Jews and Gentiles* was broken down in Jesus. We could say that *religiously*, there is no longer a distinction in Christ, whereas *culturally* every ethnic group is free to express its own culture as long as Scripture is not contradicted. But it is not always easy to separate the cultural from the religious elements of Jewishness, because rabbinic and Old Testament ceremonies and worship forms are utilized both religiously by Orthodox Jews and culturally by secular Jews. For example, an Orthodox Jew may observe Passover as a way to remember what God did in bringing us out of Egypt; for secular Jews, Passover becomes a cultural holiday (like the American holiday of Thanksgiving) to remember some Jewish history, visit with the family and eat.

Further, while the separateness of Israel and the Gentiles has been radically abolished in Christ, many Christians have historically believed the Scripture still teaches an ongoing uniqueness to the Jewish people. How are both facets to be resolved in terms of the congregational issue?[16]

Though these questions continue to be debated, the fact is that today the debate is largely theoretical. The whole question of whether there should be separate congregations for Jewish believers has, particularly in North America, become a non-issue, due to the fact that most Messianic congregations are comprised of Jews and Gentiles. In other words, these congregations are far from exclusive in their composition.

Instead we find ourselves with another question: Why do so many Gentiles want to worship in what they perceive is a Jewish way? We don't find a similar phenomenon with other ethnic groups. One doesn't find groups of Anglos who want to worship Korean style proclaiming that they are a "Korean church" nor groups of Caucasians attempting to worship like African-Americans. It is one thing for non-Jewish Christians to join a congregation led by Jewish believers with a substantial Jewish membership, just as one might find a few Anglos who for one reason or another attend a Chinese church. But what are we to make of non-Jews calling themselves "Messianic rabbis," heading congregations of mostly (or only) non-Jews, in areas of the country where few Jews live, who are attempting to worship in a Jewish mode?[17]

One can discern various motivations as to why some non-Jews seek to adopt Jewish practices:

• Some non-Jews have a romantic view of the Jewish people and assume that rabbis are the custodians of ancient wisdom that the Church has lost. While rabbinic Judaism can provide insights in the areas of ethics and biblical understanding, the fact is that rabbinic Judaism is the creation of the rabbis following the events of A.D.70. It is a post-biblical religion whose theology diverges in crucial ways from biblical theology. Its authority structure relies on the decisions of rabbis and it is a faith that denies the Messiahship of Jesus, the Incarnation and the possibility that God is a Trinity. The rabbis of today are not custodians of ancient wisdom that dates to the foundation of the world; what they are custodians of is the past two thousand years of Jewish legal and community decision-making. Incidentally, this kind of romanticized idea about Jewish people comes close to home. Often, Jews for Jesus receives phone calls or letters from people with a Bible question, convinced that we must have special expertise simply because we are Jewish. It may surprise them when we respond that they would do well to check a good Bible commentary; Jewishness is no guarantee that someone can explain a verse in the Bible, but good scholarship is!

• There are those who believe that by worshiping in Jewish style, they are returning to the worship of the "original Church," which is thought to be purer and unadulterated by so-called "pagan" additions. For example, there are those non-Jews who look at the cultural traditions of Christmas and Easter celebrations and expect that those traditions will be excised in the Messianic congregation model. However, it is never the case that by worshiping in a Messianic congregation, one can worship in a first-century manner, since the early Christians worshiped at the Temple in the context of priesthood and sacrifices.

• Some people have a personal need for structure and liturgy that Jewish tradition seems to provide, not just in a worship service but in daily life. While some segments of the Church could learn much from Jewish practice in areas such as ethics, family life and celebration, the use of art and ritual in reinforcing biblical truths, etc.,[18] there are certainly models within the traditional church that offer liturgy and structure.

A Messianic congregation comprised largely or entirely of Gentiles might be sincere in its appreciation for the Jewishness of the gospel, but it is misguided for them to attempt to worship like Jews and to adopt Jewish practices as their way of life. This is not to say that churches or individual Christians who appreciate the Jewish roots of their faith in Christ shouldn't, for example, celebrate Passover and incorporate the New Testament teaching from the Last Supper story. At Jews for Jesus, we actually encourage that kind of supportive involvement.

CONCLUSION
Messianic congregations vary as widely as do churches. Before attending or endorsing a particular Messianic congregation, it would be helpful to ask the following questions:

1. Does it have a statement of faith that is recognizably evangelical, especially regarding the deity of Jesus, the Trinity and the authority of the whole of Scripture?
2. Does it advocate mandatory keeping of the Law of Moses as a means of salvation or as a path to greater spirituality?
3. Is the leadership trained at a recognized institution or through a reputable course of study? Is the teaching sound and the Body life healthy?
4. Does the congregation seek to maintain ties to the rest of the Body of Christ?
5. Does it have a valid reason for existing (providing a context for Jewish believers and interested non-Jews to worship) or does it seem to be comprised largely of non-Jews who are acting Jewish?

6. Does it maintain that all Jewish believers should be worshiping in Messianic congregations and therefore that Jewish believers need to "come out of the church?"
7. Does it believe in evangelism and have an effective outreach program?

Jews for Jesus has good relationships with many Messianic congregations around the U.S. and internationally. In fact, many of our own staff attend Messianic congregations. We would be happy to recommend a congregation if you contact our Ministry-at-Large office at 415.864.2600 ext. 125 or mal60@aol.com.

As for recommending a Messianic congregation to a Jewish believer, there are many Jewish believers who would certainly benefit from attending a Messianic congregation; some very much enjoy the familiarity of such a service and would like their children to have the experience of a service that emphasizes their Jewish identity as well as faith in Christ.

For others, a Bible-believing church would be more suitable. Some Jewish believers would be more comfortable attending the church of whoever led them to the Lord. Or, they might have a non-Jewish spouse who comes from a particular Christian tradition that they'd like to further explore.

Don't assume that being Jewish automatically means that a Jewish believer in Jesus wants to attend a Messianic congregation. However, if a Jewish believer you know expresses the desire to attend a local Messianic congregation and you know one you can recommend, do so. If the only one you know of is unbiblical in doctrine or seriously deficient in some other way, affirm to your friend his or her Jewishness, but point out where the congregation falls short of a biblical standard and help them find another congregation if possible.

If you are not Jewish and are thinking of attending a Messianic congregation, ask yourself why. Your reasons may be good ones: for instance, you appreciate the Jewishness of the gospel and want to affirm Jewish believers in their faith or you are just curious to see what Jewish style worship and teaching are like. But if it's because you wish that you were Jewish or you think there is something inherently more spiritual about Jewish forms of worship, then those are not good motivations. In general, the principle "bloom where you are planted" is a good one. If your present congregation is fine, then stay there. Perhaps you can help them learn to appreciate the Jewishness of Jesus more!

FURTHER READING

Rosen, Ruth. *Following Y'shua.* San Francisco: Purple Pomegranate Productions, 2001.

Wasserman, Jeffrey S., *Messianic Jewish Congregations: Who Sold This Business to the Gentiles?* Lanham, MD: University Press of America, 2000.

Kjær-Hansen, Kai. *Joseph Rabinowitz and the Messianic Movement: The Herzl of Jewish Christianity.* Edinburgh: The Handsel Press; and Grand Rapids, MI: Eerdmans, 1995. A detailed and fascinating look at Rabinowitz and his "Israelites of the New Covenant," a precursor to today's Messianic congregations.

Zimmerman, Martha. *Celebrating Biblical Feasts: In Your Home or Church.* Grand Rapids: Bethany House, 2004.

Schiffman, Michael. *Return from Exile: The Re-Emergence of the Messianic Congregational Movement.* Columbus, OH: Teshuvah Publishing Co., 1990. Valuable for survey information on some 30 Messianic congregations, but now dated as the survey was conducted in the 1980s.

Baron, David. *Messianic Judaism; or Judaising Christianity*. London: Morgan & Scott; Hebrew Christian Testimony to Israel, 1911. Shows there is nothing new under the sun. The same pros and cons of Messianic congregations are debated today, but there is far more sympathy now than Baron expresses to the idea of a congregation worshiping in a culturally Jewish manner. But, like Baron, most would still consider it unbiblical for a congregation to be composed exclusively of Jews. Accessible at: www.lcje.net/history

Facts & Myths About the Messianic Congregations in Israel: A Survey Conducted by Kai Kjær-Hansen and Bodil F. Skjøtt. Jerusalem: Published by the United Christian Council in Israel in cooperation with the Caspari Center for Biblical and Jewish Studies, 1999. Appeared as *Mishkan* 30-31, 1999.

Jews for Jesus takes a stand in favor of both Messianic congregations and evangelical churches. See the following articles:

Brickner, David. "Why I Support Messianic Congregations." *Jews for Jesus Newsletter*, September 2004. http://www.jewsforjesus.org/publications/newsletter/2004_09/whyisupport

Brickner, David. "Jews for Jesus and the Church." *Jews for Jesus Newsletter*, February 2000. http://www.jewsforjesus.org/publications/newsletter/2000_02/jewsforjesusandthechurch

Brickner, David. "What About Jews for Jesus and Messianic Congregations?" *Mishpochah Message*, Fall 1993. http://www.jewsforjesus.org/publications/havurah/mm93_10/congregations

Rosen, Moishe. "Choosing Between a Local Church and a Messianic Congregation." *Mishpochah Message*, Spring 1989.

http://www.jewsforjesus.org/publications/havurah/mm89_0
4/churchcong

For an article on Messianic Jews attending and pastoring
Christian churches, see "To the Jew First and Also to the Gentile,"
Havurah 8:2:
http://www.jewsforjesus.org/publications/havurah/8_2/jewfirst

For a directory of Messianic congregations, see
www.messianictimes.com or www.yashanet.com

Notes
1. For the history of this movement, see Kai Kjær-Hansen, *Joseph
Rabinowitz and the Messianic Movement: The Herzl of Jewish
Christianity.* Edinburgh: The Handsel Press; and Grand Rapids, MI:
Eerdmans, 1995.
2. Zeidman, Morris, "Relationship of the Jewish Convert to the
Christian Church," pp. 87-92 in *Christians and Jews: A Report of the
Conference on the Christian Approach to the Jews, Atlantic City,
New Jersey, May 12-15, 1931* (New York; London: International
Committee on the Christian Approach to the Jews; International
Missionary Council, 1931).
3. Kaplan, Jonathan. "A Brief History of Presbyterian Ministry
Among Jewish People: 1820-2001." Available at:
www.theologymatters.com/TMIssues/Kaplan01.PDF. Emmanuel
began in 1915 as an interdenominational Jewish mission, though
Jewish Presbyterians were associated with it from the beginning.
4. On the other hand, a Hebrew Christian congregation was formed
in Kishinev in 1928, after Rabinowitz was gone from the scene, and
in this case it arose from an exodus of Jewish believers from the
local Baptist church.
5. It was not a new term. "Messianic Judaism" had been a phrase
used and argued over for decades, usually referring to an expression
of Christian faith that involved keeping the Law, albeit voluntarily,
and retaining many traditional Jewish forms of life and worship.
6. Hence, dating from those years, we have the Hebrew Union

College in Cincinnati, Hebrew National hot dogs, and innumerable Hebrew Homes for the Aged and similar social service agencies.

7. For an interesting take on this, see "Tough Jews: A Dissent" by Andrew Furman at www.tikkun.org

8. This point was argued against in 1911 by David Baron, who said that Jews were unlike any other nation, and thus one could not extend the validity of an ethnic church to Jews as one could to other ethnic groups. (See Further Reading).

9. Perlman, Susan. "Statistically Speaking: What's New in Jewish Community Demographics," *Havurah* 6:1, 2003. (http://www.jewsforjesus.org/publications/havurah/6_1/statistics), where the estimate of 30,000-75,000 Jewish believers in the United States is given.

10. Kravitz, Bentzion, *The Jewish Response to Missionaries Counter-Missionary Handbook* (Los Angeles: Jews for Judaism, 2001), p. 9. "According to a 1990 Council of Jewish Federations population study, over 600,000 Jews in North America alone identify with some type of Christianity." A mediating figure of 100,000 is given by the Jewish Community Relations Council Task Force on Missionaries and Cults (http://www.tfmc.us): "More than 100,000 American Jews have been converted by missionary groups in the past 20 years, and a disproportionate number of Jews have joined cults."

11. "More than three hundred" in the U.S. is a figure given by Louis Goldberg, "Introduction: The Rise, Disappearance, and Resurgence of Messianic Congregations," p. 25 in *How Jewish is Christianity? Two Views on the Messianic Movement*, ed. Louis Goldberg (Grand Rapids: Zondervan, 2003). In 1996 Jeffrey S. Wasserman surveyed 200 messianic congregations in the U.S. and Canada for his thesis, now the book *Messianic Jewish Congregations: Who Sold This Business to the Gentiles?* (Lanham, MD: University Press of America, 2000), p. 74.

12. Wasserman writes: "My survey showed 60% Gentile membership [in the messianic congregations surveyed]. Schiffman's 1987 survey revealed Gentile membership between 75% and 50%." Wasserman, *Messianic Jewish Congregations*, p. 100, note 25.

13. In Michael Schiffman's 1980s survey of 30 Messianic congregations (see Further Reading), "most ... have percentages of Jewish membership between twenty-five to fifty percent" (Schiffman, p. 119), which means 50-75% Gentile membership. Wasserman came up with 60% Gentile membership (Wasserman, p. 110, n. 25).

14. Winner, Lauren F., *Girl Meets God: A Memoir*, Random House, 2003.

15. See Ortiz, Manuel, *One New People: Models for Developing a Multiethnic Church* (Downers Grove: InterVarsity Press, 1996), p. 147-48.

16. These are not always easy questions to resolve. We would affirm the propriety (and often, the wisdom) of Jewish believers being free to worship in a Jewish way, a different question from whether "separate" congregations should be formed. And regarding the idea of multi-ethnic congregations, one could after all argue that even a congregation made up of Jewish people could be multi-ethnic, if it were a matter of bringing together Russian Jews, Ethiopian Jews, Sephardic Jews, and European Jews each with their own kind of worship and their own mutual mistrusts to overcome.

17. See "The Phenomenon: Gentiles in Synagogues," chapter 6 in Stan Telchin, *Messianic Judaism is Not Christianity: A Loving Call to Unity* (Grand Rapids: Chosen Books, 2004) and also Karabelnik, Chapter Four, "Dealing with the Foreigner in our Midst: Reactions to Gentiles." (See chapter 1.3, Further Reading).

18. In *Mudhouse Sabbath* (Paraclete Press, 2003), a recent book by Lauren Winner, she explores just these kinds of learning areas—but the rationale for the author living "Jewishly" while maintaining Christian faith is that she was raised as an Orthodox Jew.

Chapter Three
Voluntary Associations

INTRODUCTION

Voluntary associations, comprised of like-minded individuals meeting for a common purpose, have always played a prominent role in American life, and this includes the life of both the American church and the Jewish community. From the YMCA to InterVarsity Christian Fellowship, Christian voluntary associations—what some might call fellowship organizations, but which have larger goals than simply fellowship—have been formed to meet the special needs of specific groups. The concerns of various ethnic groups within the Church have also been addressed by voluntary associations such as Chinese or Korean Christian fellowships for college students.

The Jewish community has a rich history of voluntary associations, such as the *landsmanshaftn*, the immigrant associations which were once active on the Lower East Side of New York City, and which functioned as would modern support and relief groups or networks.[1]   Hillel, the campus group for Jewish students, is another example of a voluntary association.

Jewish believers in Jesus likewise have developed voluntary organizations to address common concerns, share common interests and provide mutual support.

A HISTORY OF MESSIANIC VOLUNTARY ORGANIZATIONS

The early history of voluntary organizations among Jewish believers is sketchy. In 1903, German Jewish Christian pastor Louis Meyer wrote a one-paragraph summary of the nineteenth century attempts to form such "brotherhoods,"

as he called them. Meyer mentioned ten such groups that
existed between 1823 and 1887, each of which "were
failures, and none existed more than two years."[2] He also
noted that some of them consisted of non-Jews, perhaps
foreshadowing a similar situation in the modern Messianic
congregations.[3] But he really gives nothing but a few
names and dates. Jewish believer Harcourt Samuel, who
was a pastor and General Secretary of the International
Hebrew Christian Alliance, goes back to 1813 in his very
brief recap of such organizations.[4]

The main catalysts that led to the formation of Jewish Christian
voluntary associations seem to have come towards the end of
the 19th century, when the rise of Jewish national consciousness
intersected with the experiences of Jewish believers within the
Church to produce a new dynamic, particularly in Britain and
America. On the one hand, the rise of Zionism and the influx of
Jewish immigrants to America created a milieu in which Jewish
Christians asserted their Jewish identity while affirming their
faith as Christians. On the other hand, and perhaps due to this
very assertion, Jews who believed in Jesus were not always
comfortable or accepted within the church.

The first voluntary organization that lasted any length of time
was the Hebrew Christian Alliance of Great Britain, founded
by Dr. Carl Schwartz in 1866. It met every two weeks,
produced two publications, *The Scattered Nation* and *Jewish
Christian Magazine* and grew steadily until the death of Dr.
Schwartz four years later. It wasn't until 1882 that the
Hebrew Christian Prayer Union was formed, which dwindled
down in numbers after 14 years and in 1901 was amalgamated
with the Hebrew Christian Alliance.

Some Jewish believers were looking to do more than assert their
ethnic identity; they advocated for voluntarily continuing some

of the religious observances of traditional rabbinic Judaism. In 1901, a certain Dr. E. S. Niles of New England convened the "Hebrew Messianic Conference," which had an attendance of 25 and advocated keeping the Law of Moses as a means of evangelism to Orthodox Jews. Others had substantial disagreements with this approach and undertook to form their own committee, which Louis Meyer was appointed to head.

Meyer's committee convened in 1903 in Maryland with a variety of viewpoints represented, especially over the matter of keeping the Law (following the commandments found in the first five books of the Old Testament, traditionally enumerated as 613), advocated in particular by John Mark Levy of London.[5] Yet there was also an underlying call for unity among the participants and a delineation of the benefits to be derived from an alliance of Jewish Christians: a witness to the uniqueness of Israel in God's plan; an influence in reaching other Jews with the gospel; and a positive influence upon the Church.

It took another 12 years, but in 1915 the Hebrew Christian Alliance of America (HCAA) was founded, followed by the establishment of the International Hebrew Christian Alliance (IHCA) in London in 1925.[6] Under their auspices, various other national Hebrew Christian alliances came into being.

In the 1970s, the self-perception of many Jewish believers, especially of the younger generation, changed to reflect the attitude of many other Jewish youth; there were more overt expressions of Jewishness, and people expressed more pride in being Jewish—much of this stemming from the rise of the State of Israel and especially Israel's stunning victory in the 1967 Six-Day War. With this change in self-perception came a change in self-designation—"Messianic Jew" became the description of choice, replacing the earlier "Hebrew-Christian"—and a change in the name of the HCAA. In 1975, by popular vote, the name became the Messianic Jewish Alliance of America (MJAA). Similarly, the International Hebrew Christian Alliance is today the International Messianic Jewish Alliance.

VOLUNTARY ASSOCIATIONS TODAY

The purposes of the Messianic Jewish Alliance of America (MJAA) are currently stated as the following:

1. To testify to the large and growing number of Jewish people who believe that Yeshua (Jesus) is the promised Jewish Messiah and Savior of the world.
2. To bring together Jews and non-Jews who have a shared vision for Jewish revival.
3. Most importantly, to introduce our Jewish brothers and sisters to the Jewish Messiah Yeshua.[7]

The trademark of the MJAA is the annual summer "Messiah Conference," held on the campus of Messiah College in Grantham, Pennsylvania. These vibrant affairs host a variety of speakers, bring in Israeli or other Jewish-style music groups, and include animated discussions and workshops, not to mention jam-packed plenary sessions. For many Jewish believers, a Messiah Conference was the first time they met large numbers of other Jews from around the world who also believe in Jesus. Throughout the year there are also regional MJAA conferences taking place, which are more intimate.

One does not need to be Jewish to join the MJAA or attend the Messiah Conference. Non-Jews can join as "honored associates." The MJAA website encourages non-Jewish people to join: "Both Jewish and non-Jewish believers in Yeshua are welcome to join the MJAA, from churches as well as Messianic congregations and synagogues. Each person plays a specific role in this prophetic ministry." All members pay yearly dues and in return get discounts on admission to the Messiah Conference.

The MJAA is governed by an executive committee that oversees the various ministries of the MJAA, which include relief efforts for Russian and Ethiopian Jews as well as the poor in Israel, and a Young Messianic Jewish Alliance (YMJA), which "seeks to establish and develop ministry to Messianic Single Adults, college and career groups, young married couples, and teen groups."

As for the IMJA, there are today some 14 countries comprised within the membership.[8] Joel Chernoff is the President, Paul Liberman the Executive Secretary and John Fischer and Natalio Krauthamer are Vice-Presidents.[9] The IMJA gives this description of itself:

> Membership in the IMJA is open to all Jewish believers in Yeshua who accept the Word of God as contained in the Old and New Covenants, and fellowship with other believers in a community of faith. Non Jewish believers who identify with the ministry of the IMJA are associate members and play an important and vital role in God's work through this ministry.[10]

Furthermore,

> Some of the world-wide ministries of the International Messianic Jewish Alliance include . . .
> • Bringing relief to any Jewish believer or group who has been ostracized because of his or her faith in Yeshua
> • Establishing alliances in every region of the world where there is a community of Jewish believers
> • Fostering the spiritual growth of every Jewish believer in such a way that they will live a life for the Glory of God.
> • Providing assistance to churches in restoring Jewishness of their faith and an understanding of the Jewish people.[11]

Over the years, the Alliances have attempted to meet the needs of Jewish believers around the world. Of particular note is the help the International Alliance extended to Jewish believers fleeing Hitler's Germany and to those seeking to make *aliyah* (immigrate to Israel) after the Second World War. The current direction of the MJAA appears to focus on humanitarian projects (e.g., The Joseph Project) as their primary way to "introduce our Jewish brothers and sisters" to Jesus.

In its modern history, the MJAA has become closely identified with Beth Yeshua, a vigorous Messianic congregation in the Philadelphia area. The vision and steering leadership for the MJAA for over three decades has been actively led by the leaders of that congregation, first Martin Chernoff and today his son, David. Joel Chernoff, David's brother, is the current General Secretary of the MJAA.

Curiously, while essential elements of theology are becoming a major issue among some Messianic congregational umbrella groups (see chapter 2.5), not so in the MJAA (nor the IMJA) whose theological statement of faith could be accepted by any evangelical Christian where it talks about the person of Christ and the nature of God. If there is a point of departure in which some Jewish believers feel the Alliance does not represent them, or which departs from traditional evangelical Christian understandings, it is in the area of practical theology. The Alliance, as it exists today,

- Is strongly in favor of Jewish believers attending Messianic congregations rather than mainstream churches.[12]
- Believes that it is incumbent upon Jewish believers to observe the Jewish holidays, as written in their statement of faith under the rubric of "Messianic Judaism": "We observe and celebrate the Jewish Holy Days given by God to Israel, with their fulfillment in and through the Messiah Yeshua."[13]

The organization is today strongly charismatic in its theological orientation; one of the MJAA's humanitarian programs, The Joseph Project, is said to have originated by a prophecy.[14] One writer has characterized the dual emphases of the MJAA as being "restoration" (returning to an allegedly first-century mode of faith, with later expressions being seen as impure accretions) and "revival" (in which the current move of Jews to the person of Jesus is related to prophecies of the end times and of the restoration of the nation of Israel).[15]

PHILOSOPHICAL ISSUES
In the early days of the Jewish Christian voluntary associations, the main obstacles to unity included (1) theology, particularly how appropriate it was for Jewish believers to continue observing the Law; and (2) social rivalries, especially between the wealthier, more assimilated German Jews vs. the poorer, more traditional Eastern European Jews.

The issues discussed among Jewish believers today are rather different. Most would probably be in agreement that Jewish believers can choose to keep whatever aspects of the Law and rabbinic tradition they like (as long as they don't violate biblical principles). A hundred years ago, some Jewish believers were glad to be free from what they saw as rabbinic burdens imposed by Orthodox Judaism; today, tradition and Law are often viewed within today's multi-ethnic world, not as rabbinic burdens, but as entree points into understanding one's roots and culture and as identity markers.

While the MJAA and the IMJA have been the main voluntary associations for Jewish believers for many decades, a new organization, the International Jewish Evangelical Fellowship (IJEF) was created as a conscious counterpoint to certain trends in the Messianic movement.[16] It is headed by Baruch Maoz, who is on the staff of a British-based Jewish mission,

Christian Witness to Israel, and also pastors the Grace and Truth Assembly in Israel. IJEF members particularly raise cautions with regard to incorporating rabbinic tradition, and they support the participation of Jewish believers in churches rather than Messianic congregations. The four "goals and purposes" of the IJEF as stated on their website are:

1. To promote a clear presentation of the Gospel to our people, unencumbered with rabbinic religious authority, and in terms our people can understand.
2. To call upon, encourage and assist Jewish Christians to be an active part of local Christian churches, rather than of ethnically and culturally focused congregations.
3. To create an alternative to Messianic Judaism by encouraging Jewish Christians to maintain, cultivate and express their Jewish national identity in cross-congregational contexts rather than within the context of church life and worship, and by inculcating in Jewish Christians an affection and a respect for the work of God in and through the Church throughout the ages.
4. To create a distinctly Jewish Christian voice that will address the church, the world and our people.[17]

The IJEF has sponsored annual conferences since 2003 and has produced a series of papers. It is too early to say what influence the IJEF will bring.

CONCLUSION
Much like in the Christian community, there is no voluntary organization that meets the needs and concerns of all Jewish believers in Jesus and "unites" them all. This should not be surprising; Christian unity is rarely achieved organizationally.

As part of the Messianic movement, the MJAA represents some Jewish believers, not all; in fact it would be safe to say that the majority of Jewish believers are not formal members. It calls itself "the largest association of Messianic Jewish believers in Yeshua (Jesus) in the world," but that, after all, is different than representing all Jewish believers. And in its development from the early days when it was the Hebrew Christian Alliance, it has come to represent primarily a charismatic form of expression, with an emphasis on restoration, as well as a "Messianic congregation only" position in regards to where its members should worship. Its agenda, too, is rather different than in the early days. But interestingly, a look back suggests that at no point in its history did the Alliance represent a broad base of Jewish followers of Jesus. Harcourt Samuel said of even the earlier IHCA, "Regretfully, only a small percentage of Jewish believers have become members."[18] This is very instructive, because it underscores the fact that no one can hope for one organization to be all things to all people, nor was there ever a "golden age" when Jewish Christians were all united under one banner. However, there remains a family feeling among many in the voluntary associations and the missions that is, perhaps, a more important mark of unity than organizational membership.

FURTHER READING

Karabelnik, Gabriela. "Competing Trends in Messianic Judaism: The Debate Over Evangelicalism." Unpublished senior thesis, Department of Religious Studies, Yale University, 2002. Compares and contrasts the MJAA and the UMJC (the latter discussed in Chapter 1.4).

Warnock, James. "All These Efforts were Failures: Alliances of Hebrew Christians." Paper presented at the Lausanne Consultation on Jewish Evangelism (North America), 2001. Available as a PDF download at: http://www.lcje.net/papers/2001/Warnock.pdf

Samuel, Harcourt. "The History of the International Hebrew Christian Alliance," *Mishkan: A Theological Forum on Jewish Evangelism* 14 (1991), pp. 74-79.

Winer, Robert I. *The Calling: The History of the Messianic Jewish Alliance of America 1915-1990*. Wynnewood, PA: Messianic Jewish Alliance of America, 1990. Contains much valuable historical information and primary quotes, but highly colored by the author's enthusiasm for the current MJAA: "the true calling of the Alliance [has been] unfulfilled until my generation." Unfortunately too, in the primary source material, he has chosen to replace terms used by the original authors, using "Jewish believers" instead of the original "Hebrew Christians," etc.—markedly lessening their value as historical evidence. Even so, there's a great deal of value in the sources he has brought together. But a more objective history has yet to be written.

ONLINE RESOURCES
Messianic Jewish Alliance of America: http://www.mjaa.org
International Messianic Jewish Alliance: http://www.imja.com
International Jewish Evangelical Fellowship: http://www.ijef.org

Digital Jewish Missions History Project: http://www.lcje.net/history. Here you can find the *Minutes of the First Hebrew-Christian Conference of the United States* from 1903.

Notes
1. See Soyer, Daniel, *Jewish Immigrant Associations and American Identity in New York, 1880-1939* (Harvard University Press, 1997) and the brief review by Leonard Dinnerstein at http://www.24hourscholar.com/p/articles/mi_m2082/is_4_61/ai_56909109
2. Meyer, Louis. "Hebrew Christian Brotherhood in America," *The Jewish Era*, April 15, 1903, p. 65.

3. See Chapter 1.2.

4. See Samuel, Harcourt. "The History of the International Hebrew Christian Alliance," *Mishkan: A Theological Forum on Jewish Evangelism* 14 (1991), p. 74. See also the survey in Warnock, James, "'All These Efforts Were Failures': Alliances of Hebrew Christians." Lausanne Consultation on Jewish Evangelism, North America, 2001. Warnock's paper is available at http://www.lcje.net/papers/2001/Warnock.pdf

5. *Minutes of the First Hebrew Christian Conference of the United States* (Mountain Lake Park, MD, 1903), pp. 40-51, section entitled, "The Scripture Method of Preaching the Gospel 'to the Jew first,'" by Mark Levy.

6. For a history of the HCAA (today the MJAA), see Winer, Robert I. *The Calling: The History of the Messianic Jewish Alliance of America 1915-1990*. Wynnewood, PA: Messianic Jewish Alliance of America, 1990. The IHCA's story is briefly recounted in Samuel, "History," cited above. Both were authored by those involved in their particular organizations. For an outsider's view of the HCAA/MJAA along with the UMJC (see chapter 1.4), see Gabriela Karabelnik, "Competing Trends in Messianic Judaism: The Debate Over Evangelicalism," unpublished senior thesis, Department of Religious Studies, Yale University, 2002.

7. http://mjaa.org/mjaa.html

8. http://www.imja.com/affiliated.html

9. http://www.imja.com/execom.html

10. http://www.imja.com/Intro2.html

11. Ibid.

12. "Should Jews really attempt to assimilate into churches and forego their Jewish identity when they choose to put their faith in the Jewish Messiah? Messianic Judaism answers, 'No!'" (http://mjaa.org/mj.html). Its statement of faith is integrated with the statement of faith of its sister organization, The International Alliance of Messianic Congregations and Synagogues (http://mjaa.org/StatementOfFaith.html).

13. Ibid.

14. "On the morning of February 13, 1996, the Lord sent a strong prophetic word to the General Secretary of the Messianic Jewish Alliance of America (MJAA). This message was written down and

according to Scriptural standards and confirmed by the leadership of the MJAA and various Christian leaders outside of the MJAA. As a result, the Joseph Project was born." See http://josephproject.org/

15. See Karabelnik, various places.
16. http://www.ijef.org
17. http://www.ijef.org/about/goals.php
18. Samuel, "History," p. 79.

Chapter Four
The Umbrella Organizations

INTRODUCTION

In the 1970s and following, as Messianic congregations proliferated amid much advocacy and encouragement in some quarters, there also emerged moves to form congregational associations for the purposes of mutual encouragement, accountability and pooling of resources.

This, of course, was nothing new in the history of congregations and synagogues. All sorts of structures, from denominations to loosely affiliated fellowships, have characterized Christian churches and the various branches of Judaism. For the most part, the Messianic congregational umbrella groups have avoided trying to become denominations, but neither have they been completely unstructured.

It should be noted that some Messianic congregations have been planted by existing church denominations and look primarily to their denomination for support. Most of the congregations that are part of one of the umbrella groups mentioned in this chapter have been independently formed or planted by a Jewish mission rather than by a church denomination. Finally, it should be noted that some Messianic congregations do not belong to an umbrella group at all. So just as the MJAA (Messianic Jewish Alliance of America) cannot be said to represent all Jewish believers, neither do the congregational groups represent all the Messianic congregations. However, a majority of all Messianic congregations belong to one of these two groups.

In this chapter we will also look at an umbrella group formed for Jewish missions, the Lausanne Consultation on Jewish Evangelism.

MESSIANIC JEWISH CONGREGATIONAL UMBRELLA GROUPS

While the idea of voluntary associations for Jewish believers goes back to the early 19th century, the oldest of the congregational umbrella groups was formed in 1979. It is called the Union of Messianic Jewish Congregations (UMJC). According to one history of the UMJC/MJAA by a Messianic Jewish leader, the UMJC was created as a spin-off group by some in the MJAA who did not take under advisement the call of Martin Chernoff, then-president of the MJAA, to delay forming such an organization until more maturity and growth had been evidenced by the various congregations.[1]

It was not until 1986 that the MJAA itself officially founded another umbrella group—the International Alliance of Messianic Congregations and Synagogues (IAMCS). The IAMCS has come to function as "essentially the pastoral arm of the MJAA."[2] There was tension between the two groups for some time, until they officially reconciled in 1994, with the signing of the *UMJC/MJAA Agreement of Reconciliation and Commitment.*[3]

The two umbrella groups agree to disagree in some theological and practical areas.[4] Both groups acknowledge current and historic ties to evangelicalism, yet both seek to emphasize their Jewishness. Some have observed that the IAMCS is more willing to be openly identified with evangelicalism[5] while the UMJC is seen as more concerned with maintaining ties to the Jewish community.[6] Some would describe the UMJC as less charismatic than the IAMCS and more interested in keeping rabbinic forms and customs.

Jewish believer Gabriela Karabelnik elaborates in her thesis:

> While the UMJC acknowledges certain ties to evangelicalism historically and theologically, a

conscious and increasing disassociation from it is taking place. Within the UMJC, restorationism[7] takes on a different form or is minimized altogether, as is the intense focus on the end time [both of which are characteristic of the MJAA/IAMCS]. The Union seeks to enter into dialogue with Jewish traditions over the ages, valuing rabbinic contributions and often adopting their rituals and liturgy to a greater extent and sometimes without specific Messianic adaptation or justification. Mosaic law and Jewish tradition are kept not so much to point to Messianic content within it, but because they are inherently valuable as God's law and as tokens of Jewish heritage. Furthermore, large parts of Mosaic Law are considered to be a continued obligation for Messianic Jews and not merely a matter of personal conscience. All of these distinguishing marks of the UMJC serve the central goal of building bridges with the Jewish community by creating a maximally "authentic" and "credible" form of Judaism.[8]

To that end, theologically, the UMJC leadership has allowed some questionable ideas to come under its rubric (see chapter 2.5 for more on this). This has resulted in some congregations pulling out of the UMJC.

While the UMJC and IAMCS are the two major congregational umbrella groups, there have been others. In 1986, there was another group formed with a non-charismatic emphasis called the Fellowship of Messianic Congregations (FMC), led by Louis Lapides, pastor of Beth Ariel Fellowship in Sherman Oaks, California. The FMC emphasized unity through doctrinal maturity. Its four purposes were stated as:

1. To encourage and assist in the establishment and growth of Messianic congregations.

2. To develop cooperation among like-minded congregations through their leaders.
3. To represent a biblically and theologically sound Messianic faith to the body of the Messiah and to society at large.
4. To carry the message of redemption to the entire world by practicing and promoting the priority of the Gospel to the Jew first and also to the gentile.[9]

Due to its small size and limited membership and resources, the FMC disbanded in the late nineties.

In 2003, the Association of Messianic Congregations (AMC) was formed. Some have regarded it as the successor association to the FMC. Their purpose statement reads as follows: "The Association of Messianic Congregations exists to strengthen Messianic Congregations by providing resources, teaching and fellowship that promote Biblical values, proclaims personal faith in Yeshua as the one Atonement for all humanity, and encourages worship through the diversity of Jewish expressions of faith."[10] The AMC describes itself as "grace-embracing"; its statement of faith includes the view that the Law of Moses is no longer mandatory upon Jewish or any believers to observe.[11] In addition, this group presents itself as a non-charismatic alternative to the charismatic/Pentecostal orientation of the MJAA and IAMCS. It was spearheaded by Steve Shermett, who leads the Messianic congregation Beth Sar Shalom in Tucson, Arizona and who serves as President; Pete Koziar of Baltimore's B'nai Abraham Congregation is Vice-President; Mottel Baleston who heads Messengers Messianic Jewish Fellowship in New Jersey serves as Board Secretary.[12] Of the eleven congregations listed in their online directory,[13] one is in Israel, another in Montreal, Canada and a third is in the UK. As of the writing of this booklet, an AMC-Europe is opening up under the leadership of Dr. Alan Poyner-Levison.

THEOLOGICAL AND PHILOSOPHICAL CONCERNS

As stated above, in the past few years there have been signs of ferment within the UMJC, mainly having to do with issues of theology. This has already caused some congregations to pull out of the UMJC and has raised red flags among others. This is particularly true in the area of ecclesiology, the doctrine of the Church. For more on this development, please see Chapter 2.5.

Another umbrella group that raised concerns in the past was a Maryland-based group known as the "Association of Torah-Observant Messianics" (A.T.O.M.). Torah-observant groups—which believe that keeping the Law of Moses is mandatory or spiritually necessary—are discussed in Part Two. A.T.O.M. described itself as "an international organization of followers of Yeshua who believe that the Torah is, always has been, and always will be G-d's perfect standard for our lives."[14]

The history of A.T.O.M. is a cautionary tale. In December of 1997 their statement of faith made reference to the Father, Son and Spirit, although not in standard evangelical phraseology; affirmed the inspiration of the Old and New Testaments; spoke of Yeshua as the Messiah whose death atoned for our sins; affirmed the sin nature and the need to trust in Yeshua for forgiveness. In addition it included statements on the Torah (in terms which many evangelicals could agree with) and added a charismatic-flavored statement on spiritual gifts. By 2001 the organization was known as A.T.O.N., the Association of Torah-Observant Nazarenes under the auspices of netzarim.org, a theologically heterodox organization. By 2002 Steve Heiliczer, the founder of A.T.O.M., had renounced his faith in Jesus altogether, changed his name from Steve to Yeshayahu, and published his story online.[15] His website, teshuvah.com, is now a completely Orthodox Jewish site and links to anti-missionary organizations and mainstream Jewish sites.

JEWISH MISSIONS UMBRELLA GROUPS

The Fellowship of Christian Testimonies to the Jews (FCTJ) was formed in the early 1950s by Fred Kendal and Emil Elbe. Kendal was General Director and founder of a Jewish mission called Israel's Remnant that was based in Detroit. Elbe was Superintendent of the Midwest Messianic Center in St. Louis. Meeting every one or two years at various locations in the U.S. and Canada, the FCTJ was intended for those engaged in Jewish ministry in those countries to be of mutual encouragement to one another and to exchange ideas on methods and issues in Jewish evangelism. Of particular note was its production of *Ha'Or*, an evangelistic publication used by various mission agencies for about twenty years. Fred Kendal was the first editor, followed by his son-in-law Avi Brickner in the late sixties. Brickner (father of David Brickner of Jews for Jesus) was also elected president of the FCTJ at that time.

Perhaps the most interesting moment in the history of the FCTJ was in 1970 when Jewish rabbi Sid Lawrence was invited to speak to its annual conference. When asked what the image of missionaries to the Jews was in the Jewish community, he replied that they had no image! His words served as a challenge to the various Jewish missionaries (among them Moishe Rosen, who later founded Jews for Jesus) to be more visible and effective.

The FCTJ was originally a somewhat loose association of individuals who had the right to vote on various issues. Some of the mission boards felt they did not want to see that kind of power in the hands of individuals rather than mission boards. In the early 1970s, there was discussion of making the organization to be an association of missionary societies in order to develop the kinds of standards in ethics and operations that other mission organizations shared. The FCTJ constitution was changed so that only mission boards could be members.

Around that time the FCTJ began objecting to certain trends that it saw among some in the Messianic movement. At the annual meeting in 1975, a resolution was put forth that essentially took issue with many of these trends, such as those who would declare Messianic Judaism to be a fourth branch of Judaism. The resolution was authored by Harold Sevener, then with the American Board of Missions to the Jews; William Currie, director of the American Messianic Fellowship; and Marvin Rosenthal who headed the Friends of Israel.

The FCTJ went out of existence in the 1980s. One reason for its demise was the conservatism of the organization; some of its members became closed to new approaches. Another reason was that when it stopped being an organization of individual missionaries and changed so that only mission societies could be members and vote, the attendance at the conferences dwindled to mostly mission leaders. The new constitution also required unanimous approval for all new member organizations. None was approved after the new constitution was put in place.

In a sense, the FCTJ was the forerunner to the Lausanne Consultation on Jewish Evangelism (LCJE). The story of the LCJE begins in 1980, when the Lausanne Committee for World Evangelization (LCWE) sponsored the Consultation on World Evangelization (COWE) in Pattaya, Thailand. "Reaching Jews" was one of the 17 mini-consultation groups at that event.[16] The enthusiasm of the leaders in the field of Jewish evangelism in attendance to expand the network gave rise to the formation of a task force, which became the LCJE. The basis for cooperation through the LCJE is agreement by its members to the Lausanne Covenant. Today, the LCJE is the main umbrella group for Jewish Missions.

LCJE meets for international consultations every four years, and more often on a regional basis. There are chapters in North

America, Europe, Israel, South Africa, Australia, Japan and Latin America. A quarterly, the *LCJE Bulletin*, is published to keep its members abreast of what is happening in between consultations. Many Jewish evangelism agencies, congregations engaged in Jewish evangelism, scholars and writers in the field, individual agency workers, and congregational leaders belong to the LCJE. Some Messianic congregational leaders attend LCJE conferences, and these meetings can provide a forum for dialogue between mission leaders and academic figures. A list of LCJE member organizations appears as Appendix C.

CONCLUSION

In a later chapter, we will discuss in more depth the quandaries facing congregational umbrella organizations. For now, it is important to note that the Messianic movement is still finding itself in terms of its identity, and will probably continue to struggle for some time.

FURTHER READING

Karabelnik, Gabriela, "Competing Trends in Messianic Judaism: The Debate Over Evangelicalism." Unpublished senior thesis, Department of Religious Studies, Yale University, 2002. Discusses the history of the UMJC and MJAA and highlights their distinctives.

Winer, Robert I. *The Calling: The History of the Messianic Jewish Alliance of America 1915-1990* (Wynnewood, PA: Messianic Jewish Alliance of America, 1990.) This book also has some helpful information on the formation of the IAMCS.

Lapides, Louis S. "Do We Need the Fellowship of Messianic Congregations?" *Mishkan* 6/7 (1987), pp. 121-134.

Juster, Daniel C. "The History of the Union of Messianic Jewish Congregations." *Mishkan* 2 (1985), pp. 63, 68.

ONLINE RESOURCES

Union of Messianic Jewish Congregations:
http://www.umjc.org

International Alliance of Messianic Congregations and
Synagogues: http://www.iamcs.org

The Association of Messianic Congregations:
http://www.messianicassociation.org

Lausanne Consultation on Jewish Evangelism:
http://www.lcje.net
Here you will find many of the LCJE conference papers and
the *LCJE Bulletin.*

The Lausanne Covenant:
http://www.lausanne.org/Brix?pageID=12891

Notes

1. Winer, Robert I. *The Calling: The History of the Messianic Jewish Alliance of America 1915-1990* (Wynnewood, PA: Messianic Jewish Alliance of America, 1990), p. 64.
2. Ibid. p. 65.
3. Hocken, Peter. "The Rise of Messianic Judaism," online at http://www.BaruchHaShemSynagogue.org/resources/riseofmj.html
4. One Jewish believer, writer Gabriela Karabelnik, has helpfully detailed the history and distinctives of the UMJC and the IAMCS in her thesis (see Further Reading).
5. Karabelnik observes that the MJAA/IAMCS shows "greater willingness to identify officially with evangelical movements," being "more typically evangelical/charismatic than the Union in its attitude towards theology, [and] also in its self-presentation." In contrast, "the Union is more reluctant to link itself with evangelicalism." See "Competing Trends," Part One, section "The MJAA versus the UMJC."

6. Ibid. "one of the clear goals of [the UMJC] is to identify more fully with the Jewish community, both historically and in the present."

7. At several points in her thesis, Karabelnik describes rather than defines "restorationism," e.g., "the claim that everything after Jesus was corrupt and that Messianic Jews are repristinating the biblical faith that other groups have lost." She nuances this by also describing "full" vs. "modified" restorationism.

8. Karabelnik, Chapter 5, "Facing our Brethren: Reactions to Non-Messianic Jews," section "The UMJC Challenging the 'Saved' versus 'Unsaved' Dichotomy."

9. For details on the FMC including the full text of its constitution, see Lapides, Louis S. "Do We Need the Fellowship of Messianic Congregations?" *Mishkan* 6/7 (1987), pp. 121-134.

10. http://www.messianicassociation.org/about.htm

11. http://www.messianicassociation.org/believe.htm

12. http://www.messianicassociation.org/board.htm

13. http://www.messianicassociation.org/directory.htm

14. This sounds like something that many Christians would agree with—surely everything in the Bible reflects "God's perfect standard"—but the practical outworking was something far different than what evangelical Christians would have in mind. http://web.archive.org/web/19980504010126/teshuvah.com/organizations/atom/membership.html

15. http://web.archive.org/web/20030810051135/www.teshuvah.com/articles/journey.htm

16. The document is available at: http://www.lausanne.org/Brix?pageID=14607. Jewish missions continue on the radar of the LCWE. In 2004, again meeting in Pattaya, the forum on Jewish evangelism produced "Jewish Evangelism: A Call to the Church," downloadable at: http://community.gospelcom.net/lcwe/assets/LOP60_IG31.pdf

Chapter Five
Educational Institutions

INTRODUCTION

It naturally follows from a discussion of congregations and congregational institutions, that there must exist programs to train congregational leaders as well as those in Jewish mission work. This section highlights these institutions, beginning with the Jewish mission training institutes that were birthed as early as the 18th century.

In a later chapter we will address another aspect of Messianic education: the "Hebrew Roots" teaching movement, which functions more as a vehicle for the layperson than as a means of training leaders.

EARLY EDUCATIONAL INSTITUTIONS

The first modern institution for training missionaries to the Jews is generally agreed to be the Institutum Judaicum, founded in 1728 by Professor Johann Heinrich Callenberg in the University of Halle, Germany. Callenberg was part of the German Pietist movement of the 18th century, and the Institutum was established even before the rise of modern missions. It began on quite a small scale, as an attempt to publish a Yiddish-language missionary tract. It would seem that rather than offering a formal program of studies with a set curriculum and so many years of classwork, Callenberg's Institutum fielded some 20 missionaries, provided Christian literature in several languages, and offered instruction to new Jewish believers in Jesus. But because it was connected with the University of Halle, the academic setting was serious and rigorous and "set high standards for informed and qualified missionary work."[1] The areas of study included languages (Hebrew, Yiddish) and rabbinics. The Institute lasted until 1792.

Yet even before Callenberg, suggestions were made for schools in which Jewish Studies would be taught as an adjunct to the work of convincing Jewish people that Jesus was the Messiah (the term "Jewish missions" had not yet entered the vocabulary). In the 17th century, Johann Christof Wagenseil, Professor of History at Altdorf University, detailed his plans for a Christian institute of Jewish studies, training students in the languages, in rabbinics, and in what today would be called apologetics.[2] It was partly as a result of momentum developing from Wagenseil and others that Callenberg began the Institutum Judaicum.

Around 1880, the scholar Franz Delitzsch began another Institutum Judaicum in Leipzig, Germany. Just a few short years afterwards, in 1886, a similar institute was started in Berlin by Professor H. L. Strack. By the time of the publication of the *Jewish Encyclopedia* in 1906, these institutes were still in existence as Jewish missionary training centers. In that encyclopedia, we read that:

> The institutes of Leipsic and Berlin have courses in New Testament theology with reference to the Messianic passages in the Old Testament, and they also give instruction in rabbinic literature; they further publish works helpful to their cause, as biographies of famous converts, controversial pamphlets, autobiographies of converted Jews, and occasionally scientific tracts. The Berlin institute has published Strack's "Introduction to the Talmud," his editions of some tractates of the Mishnah, and a monograph on the blood accusation. A special feature of its publications is the New Testament in Hebrew and Yiddish translations.[3]

It is apparent from this description that the curriculum was wide-ranging and that the institutes relied on recognized scholars: Strack's *Introduction to the Talmud* remains a standard work to this day, while Franz Delitzsch's writings, and especially his Hebrew translation of the New Testament, are of enduring value. Both institutes also produced periodicals.

Much of the resources of these institutes were destroyed during the Second World War. Today, the Leipzig organization has been reborn, not as a missionary training center, but as a school for the study of Judaism, and is called the Institutum Judaicum Delitzschianum, now located in Münster.

CURRENT TRENDS IN MESSIANIC EDUCATION

In the 20th and 21st centuries, the locus of Messianic Jewish or Jewish missions education has largely moved from Europe to the United States, with Israel as a secondary center. In America as well as elsewhere, modern missionaries to the Jewish people usually receive their theological education at evangelical Bible schools or seminaries, in addition to which a mission agency might have its own internal training course.

There are some Bible schools that offer Jewish studies degrees or emphases within their curricula. On the undergraduate level, Moody Bible Institute's Jewish studies program in Chicago has long been a vehicle for training missionaries to the Jewish people (though one doesn't have to be a missionary in training to enroll). The program began in 1923 as the Jewish Missions Course, which was a three-year program under the auspices of the Hebrew Christian Alliance of America before becoming part of Moody. Subjects included Hebrew and Yiddish, rabbinics, Jewish history, and Messianic prophecy, as well as Jewish holidays and customs. Solomon Birnbaum, a Jewish believer in Jesus, was the first director. In 1940, Max I. Reich took over leadership of the program, and he was succeeded in turn by Nathan J. Stone in 1946, Louis Goldberg in 1966, and Michael Rydelnik in 2001.[4] Moody's program remains the most extensive of its kind, at least in the United States. Today, in keeping with changed times, course requirements no longer include Yiddish, but have added Contemporary Jewish Literature, the Holocaust, and the History and Thought of Modern Israel, along with continuing requirements of Hebrew, Jewish history and Messianic prophecy.[5]

Shorter programs include Philadelphia Biblical University's "Friends of Israel Institute of Jewish Studies," which has been in place in Langhorne, Pennsylvania since 1996, in association with The Friends of Israel, a Jewish mission agency that originally ran the program under their own auspices from 1987-96.[6] This program is one year in duration, taught in modules and includes a study trip to Israel. Youth With a Mission (YWAM) conducts an in-depth, 12-week School of Jewish Studies and brings in respected faculty to teach its intensive courses. Also available is an additional internship in mercy ministries, intercession, education in the USA and abroad.

On the graduate level, a masters program in Jewish missions was taught at Fuller Theological Seminary's School of World Mission in the 1990s in partnership with Jews for Jesus, through which dozens of Jews for Jesus missionaries and others interested received degrees. It is no longer offered; however, Jews for Jesus has now partnered with Western Seminary in offering a Master of Arts in Specialized Ministry in Jewish Evangelism degree at their San Jose campus. The Specialized Ministry programs are intended for students seeking specialized, graduate, theological education. The program is slated to begin in the Fall of 2005. Faculty will include Tuvya Zaretsky of Jews for Jesus and Galen Peterson, who is an adjunct instructor in Intercultural Studies at Western and heads the American Remnant Mission, a Jewish outreach in the San Francisco area.

Then there is the Pasche Institute of Jewish Studies at Criswell College in Dallas, Texas, formed in 2004. It offers an M.A. in Jewish Studies as well. Named after members of First Baptist Church in Dallas, the institute's vision is "to multiply and strengthen Kingdom leaders for ministry to the Jewish people and to significantly contribute to the scholarship of Jewish studies." As of this writing, faculty include one full-time (Todd Bradley) and five adjunct (Arnold Fruchtenbaum, J. Randall Price, Michael Rydelnik, Jim Sibley and Tuvya Zaretsky).

Israel has also become a place for similar studies. In a formal, degree-granting setting, Israel College of the Bible (formerly King of Kings College) also includes Jewish studies within its bachelors and certificate programs. It offers courses in Hebrew, Russian, Amharic and English. Based in Jerusalem since 1990, this interdenominational school is accredited through the Asian Theological Association and the European Evangelical Accrediting Association. It has a student body of indigenous Israelis, as well as short-term course offerings for non-Israeli residents. Its stated purpose is "to equip and to develop leaders for serving the Lord and to provide a unique understanding of the Jewish roots of the Faith in Yeshua (Jesus)."[7]

Also in Israel, the Caspari Center is "an educational institute for academic study and training where Messianic Jews and Gentile Christians work in cooperation. The staff consists of local Israelis working together with Christians from the nations . . . The Israeli focus is in providing local believers with serious theological education and training. . . ."[8] The Caspari Center was founded in 1982 by the Norwegian Church Ministry to Israel to fill a need for Hebrew-language training.

It was named after Carl Paul Caspari (1814-1892), a Jewish believer who was professor of Old Testament at the University of Oslo and first chairman of the Committee for the Mission among the Jews in that city.

The Caspari Center functions today as a study center and think tank, offering lectures and seminars "with the possibility of academic credit," publishing the journal *Mishkan: A Forum on the Gospel and the Jewish People*, and currently sponsoring a multi-volume scholarly project, "History of the Jewish Believers in Jesus from Antiquity to the Present" under the editorship of Oskar Skarsaune, professor of church history at the Norwegian Lutheran School of Theology in Oslo. Though not a formal degree-granting institution, the Caspari Center maintains a high academic caliber in its offerings and projects.

In addition to the above institutions, various other vehicles have been created to train aspiring leaders in the Messianic movement, particularly leaders of Messianic congregations, and others who might be interested. The newest undergraduate program is the Messianic Jewish concentration offered at Nyack College in New York, as a track within the Pastoral Ministry program. Nyack's program, spearheaded by Messianic Rabbi David Rosenberg, is "designed for students who are desiring to be Rabbis of Messianic Jewish congregations. All streams of the Messianic movement will be welcomed and represented in the courses of this concentration."[9]

The Messianic Jewish Training Institute (MJTI) was established in 2002 as the training arm of the UMJC congregational leaders (see chapter 1.4 on the UMJC). MJTI has a faculty of seven, five of whom have earned doctorates. MJTI consists of two schools: The School of Jewish Studies (SJS) and the Rabbinical Ordination Institute (ROI). The School of Jewish Studies offers academic courses and concentrations in Scripture, rabbinics, theology, history, and spiritual life, all taught from a Messianic Jewish perspective. The Rabbinical Ordination Institute supplements the SJS curriculum by offering practical courses in rabbinical leadership. ROI also provides spiritual and vocational direction for rabbinical candidates. MJTI is based in Ann Arbor, Michigan. Week-long intensive courses are taught in Michigan and at regional campuses in Virginia, Connecticut and Pasadena. In addition, MJTI is linked to the Netzer David International Yeshiva in Clearwater, Florida, which is headed by Dr. John Fischer and attached to the recently accredited St. Petersburg Theological Seminary.

MJTI's stated purpose is to "serve the Messianic Jewish movement by providing advanced education and training for those seeking ordination within the UMJC." So, for instance, applicants to the rabbinical ordination program must submit "reflections on the official UMJC statement, 'Defining Messianic Judaism.'" [10]

The congregational wing of the Messianic Jewish Alliance of America, the International Alliance of Messianic Congregations and Synagogues (IAMCS), does not have a formal educational institution, but provides courses at its conferences and on tape for its members. [11] There doesn't seem to be a formal educational track for the leaders of MJAA to receive their ordination and rabbinic titles as there is for the UMJC leaders. Another institution is the Messianic Bible Institute-Yeshiva [12] in Newport News, Virginia, which is run by David Hargis, which is further discussed in the next section.

EVALUATING THE STATE OF MESSIANIC JEWISH EDUCATION

When it comes to evaluating Messianic Jewish education, it's important to keep in mind that while the programs offered are small, this does not mean they aren't quality. The question is not the size of the institution, but the value of faculty and education offered.

Missionaries to the Jewish people have typically been trained in evangelical schools and seminaries that are well established and are known for offering a high quality education. More recently, many Messianic congregational leaders have been trained through their own institutions, such as the Messianic Bible Institute-Yeshiva and MJTI, or through specialized but non-accredited courses. As these newer institutions purport to be training present and future leadership of the Messianic movement, they deserve close scrutiny.

In the case of the Messianic Bible Institute-Yeshiva, their accreditation is through the Transworld Accrediting Commission, an agency, which has been described by one writer as an "accrediting mill."[13] Yet the Institute offers degrees through correspondence courses that one would normally require accreditation for: Bachelor of Bible, Master of Divinity, Master of Theology in Messianic Studies, and Master of Theology degrees in Rabbinic Studies. Under Virginia law, they are allowed to offer such degrees. Thus the question is not one of legality, but of the value of the degrees granted. The Institute also offers ordination as a Messianic rabbi, even though, unlike the UMJC, they are not a congregational organization. Their credentials come with a peculiar disclaimer that "MBI does not make any claim that the qualifications are infallible, nor that their credentials necessarily proves the qualifications and ability of anyone to do the work of ministry."[14]

The catalog from MJTI describes an impressive array of courses whose descriptions reflect a high caliber of thought. The faculty are known to many within the Messianic movement. Some hold masters degrees and doctorates from recognized institutions. Mark Kinzer, who heads up the MJTI, holds a Ph.D. from the University of Michigan. The MJTI offers perspectives on the Jewishness of the Bible and theology that may not be found in most mainstream Christian seminaries, and also highlights particular issues (alleged anti-Semitism in the New Testament, for instance) that those ministering among Jewish people need to understand.

However, many evangelicals would describe Mark Kinzer as theologically liberal in some of his views, and indeed he espouses some very non-traditional positions, most notably on matters of ecclesiology (see chapter 2.5). The program of MJTI is stronger on Bible courses and courses on rabbinic writings than on theology. The theological categories are placed in terms that Jewish thinkers have chosen to interact on, rather than on traditional categories as taught in evangelical seminaries. That is not wrong in itself, as we should always be looking for contextual ways to present abiding truth.

However, if one is looking to find new ways of doing theology and Bible study, the least one should do is expose students to the traditional ways of thinking that they are attempting to change. It is noteworthy that while theology courses are in the MJTI catalog, the only history taught is Jewish history; the history of the Church, Christian theology and reflection are not explicitly addressed. One wonders if traditional Christian viewpoints are adequately represented.

CONCLUSION

For those interested in attending a school (or classes) to learn more about Jesus and the New Testament from a Messianic Jewish perspective, or about the Jewish backgrounds to Christianity, see if there is a local evangelical seminary or Bible college offering such a course. If you are considering attending a local Messianic "yeshiva" or an institute such as the MJTI, recognize that unless a school is properly accredited, you cannot count on earning a degree that will be generally recognized, if that is what you are after.

Whether it is a local Messianic institute or a course offered through an evangelical seminary or Bible college, learn something about the school and the faculty. Some salient questions to ask are: What is the institute's statement of faith? Do faculty members have degrees and from which institutions? What is their theological perspective? For example, are they part of the current theological ferment in the Messianic movement? Are they presenting "new" and untested approaches to Bible and theology that do not also present the traditional approaches? Would their views be considered idiosyncratic or non-evangelical were they to be subjected to scrutiny by evangelical scholars? What affiliations do they have? That is, are they members of recognized evangelical associations and agencies? Affiliations are one of the most helpful tests for an institution's general theological outlook.

Do not assume that because the instructor is Jewish or affiliated with a Messianic organization, or because they are presenting a "Jewish perspective," that they therefore have the best "take" on things. Some non-Jewish scholars have done some of the best and most enduring research on the Jewishness of the gospel. Lastly, do not assume that because a Jewish perspective is being taught, that therefore the instructor is unlocking "secrets" never before revealed. Most serious Bible scholarship is well aware of, and interacts with, the Jewish backgrounds to the New Testament.

FURTHER READING

Rosen, Moishe. "Reflections on Missionary Training." Paper delivered at the Lausanne Consultation on Jewish Evangelism of North America, 2004. Available at: http://www.lcje.net/papers/2004/rosen.doc

Dillan, Vicky. "The MBI Yeshiva and the Hargis Clan" on the Seek God website: http://www.seekgod.ca/mbiyeshiva.htm. In the genre of investigative reporting and overall a good site, but not all will agree with the theological conservatism of the author—she is opposed to "ecumenism" as well as various trends in modern evangelicalism and hence also calls Jews for Jesus, the Lausanne Consultation on Jewish Evangelism and others into question.

ONLINE RESOURCES

Educational institutions discussed above (listed alphabetically):

Caspari Center: http://www.caspari.com
Friends of Israel Institute of Jewish Studies at Philadelphia Biblical University: http://www.pbu.edu/programs/ijs/
IAMCS Yeshiva: http://www.iamcs.org/Yeshiva.php
Israel College of the Bible: http://www.israelcollege.com
Messianic Bible Institute–Yeshiva:
http://www.Messianicbureau.org/mbima/
Messianic Jewish Theological Institute (training arm for the UMJC): http://www.mjti.org/
Moody Bible Institute: http://www.moody.edu
Nyack College's Jewish Studies Concentration:
http://www.nyack.edu/2005.php?page=PMNConcentrations
The Pasche Institute: http://pascheinstitute.org/about.html
Western Seminary's program:
http://www.westernseminary.edu/AcademicPrograms/SJ/MASM.htm

Notes

1. Clark, Christopher M., *The Politics of Conversion: Missionary Protestantism and the Jews in Prussia 1728-1941.* Oxford: Clarendon Press, 1995, p. 51; and see pp. 47-57, section "The Institutum Judaicum in Halle."
2. For this and further details, see Mevorah, Barouh, "Precursors of the Pietist "Institutum Judaicum," *Immanuel* 21 (Summer 1987), pp. 99-105.

3. Deutsch, Gotthard, "Institutum Judaicum," *Jewish Encyclopedia*, 1906. Online at:
http://www.jewishencyclopedia.com/view.jsp?artid=156&letter=I

4. See Getz, Gene A., *MBI: The Story of Moody Bible Institute* (Chicago: Moody Press, 1969), pp. 101, 162.

5. http://mmm.moody.edu/GenMoody/Media/MediaLibrary/UGCatalog0406rev_3.pdf, p. 170

6. http://www.pbu.edu/programs/ijs/, with further information in the "IJS Links" section.

7. http://www.israelcollege.com/showpage.php?cat=1

8. http://www.caspari.com/about.html

9. http://www.nyack.edu/2005.php?page=PMNConcentrations

10. Catalog, p. 4, available as PDF download at http://www.mjti.org/mjti/catalog.pdf

11. http://www.iamcs.org/Yeshiva.php

12. A "yeshiva" is a traditional Jewish school of learning.

13. See discussion at http://www.seekgod.ca/mbiyeshiva.htm.

14. http://www.messianicbureau.org/mbima/

Chapter Six
Philo-Semitic Organizations*

INTRODUCTION
Christian anti-Semitism has been one of the greatest obstacles to effective Jewish evangelism over the centuries—not to mention simply being a moral evil. Though anti-Semitism existed long before there were Christians (e.g., Pharaoh and Haman), to many Jewish people, Christianity as an institution has become synonymous with the Crusades, the Inquisition, Martin Luther's anti-Jewish polemics and even Adolf Hitler. Although the Nazi regime was no friend of Christianity either, many German churches were nevertheless complicit in the events surrounding the Holocaust. On a more personal level, many older Jewish people have childhood memories of being called "Christ-killers" by people they knew who claimed to be Christians.

It is in the context of the history of anti-Semitism that a number of philo-Semitic, or for want of a better term, "Love Israel" organizations have arisen. Their goal is to show the Jewish world that true Christians who embody the spirit of Christ love the Jewish people, and to persuade Christians to support Israel. Such organizations are often perceived to be part of the Messianic Movement.

A BIT OF BACKGROUND
Demonstrations of love for Israel and the Jewish people are not new. Even in the early church, much anti-Jewish writing was directed not against Jews, but against "philo-Semitic" Christians. These Christians came from the ranks of the "God-fearers," that

(*organizations that promote a love for Israel)

is, those who already had an attraction to Judaism and the Jewish people. It is the anti-Jewish writing that has survived, but its very existence underscores the early existence of what one scholar calls a "grass-roots" philo-Semitic movement.[1]

In more recent times, modern Jewish missions arose out of a concern for the Jewish people that embraced the desire to see them come to know Christ and attempted to meet their physical needs. The Jewish perspective was, unsurprisingly, rather different. Attempts to share Christ with Jewish people were viewed as anything but acts of love. Material help, especially of a medical nature, was more welcome. However, today, at least in the West, Jewish people are well provided for, and in fact have produced a large number of physicians.

In the late 19th century, the rise of Zionism found many advocates among Christians who believed that a Jewish homeland would be a fulfillment of prophecy. Humanitarian motives played a part as well. To this day the Jewish community usually welcomes Christians who support Israel, though some question the motivations of evangelical Christians who also believe that Jewish people need to hear the gospel.

In entering a discussion of philo-Semitism, it must also be noted that during the Holocaust individual Christians often reached out to Jews, hiding them or facilitating their escape. They number among the "righteous Gentiles" that Jewish tradition honors.

Over the years, the vision and position of some philo-Semitic organizations and people have modified. When Jewish evangelism was still strongly on the agenda of Christian churches, evangelistic efforts were united with social programs to share God's love in Christ. In contrast, the newer philo-Semitic organizations have arisen at a time when many Christian denominations have openly repudiated the need for the proclamation of the gospel to Jewish people.

Even among evangelical Christians, pressure to refrain from Jewish evangelism has come from several fronts—not just the Jewish community. First, the past several decades have seen an emphasis on dialogue over what is pejoratively called "proselytism," that is, evangelism. Second, postmodernism and pluralism have influenced a softening of theological positions regarding the necessity of faith in Christ for salvation for anyone, not just for Jewish people. Third, there has been an increasingly widespread promulgation of "Two-Covenant" or "Dual-Covenant" theology— the idea that Jews already have a relationship with God through the covenant with Abraham and therefore have no need for Jesus. These forces have all combined to erode evangelical support for Jewish evangelism.[2] Consequently, the most recent expressions of love for the Jewish people tend to downplay or disavow evangelism altogether.

CURRENT PHILO-SEMITIC EFFORTS
It is with this background in mind that we look at some of the better-known philo-Semitic organizations.

The International Fellowship of Christians and Jews (IFCJ)

IFCJ has perhaps the highest profile of any of the modern philo-Semitic organizations. Unlike some of the others described below, IFCJ is headed not by Christians, but by Yechiel Eckstein, a mainstream Jewish rabbi who is not a believer in Jesus. Among the programs of the IFCJ is "Stand for Israel," which promotes prayer for Israel and Christian advocacy for the State of Israel. On an FAQ page of IFCJ's website,[3] the question is asked, "Does the Fellowship evangelize or share the gospel with those they help through their programs?" The answer: "While we affirm the right and duty of evangelical Christians to share the gospel, we are not an organization that seeks to convert people to either Christianity or Judaism. Our mission of building bridges between Christians and Jews would be compromised if we endorsed any conversion efforts."

While Rabbi Eckstein perhaps affirms the "right and duty" of sharing the gospel on his website, elsewhere he speaks of Jewish evangelism in the harshest terms: "When directed at Jews, however, Christian missions conflict with and even jeopardize the central ethic guiding Jewish life today—Jewish survival. While Christians have sought to convert Jews to Christianity for almost two millennia, after the holocaust those attempts are regarded as especially pernicious threats to Jewish survival—indeed, a form of spiritual genocide."[4]

Rabbi Eckstein is simultaneously soliciting support from evangelical Christians and isolating Jewish believers in Jesus from the support of the Church at large. Not only has he gone on record as opposed to Jewish evangelism, but he also has harsh words for Jews who follow Jesus. One writer who has studied some aspects of the Messianic movement wrote in the *Journal of Ecumenical Studies*:

> Orthodox Rabbi Yechiel Eckstein, another national participant in interfaith dialogue, believes that Messianic Jews engage in deceptive proselytizing . . . Eckstein asked, 'Is it any wonder that Jews are so deeply offended by such groups and tend to regard them as essentially no different from cults?' This author spoke with a representative of Eckstein's organization, the International Fellowship of Christians and Jews, in September, 1998, who indicated that Eckstein's position on Messianic Jews had not changed.[5]

Despite his characterization of evangelism of the Jewish people as "spiritual genocide," and his disdain for Jews who believe in Jesus,

Rabbi Eckstein is endorsed by some leading evangelical Christians. In 2003, Jews for Jesus issued a statement authored by Executive Director David Brickner, which read in part:

> Some well-known pastors and Christian leaders have either endorsed those who oppose Jewish evangelism or have carefully avoided endorsing anyone who does engage in effective gospel outreach to Jewish people. Some are flattered by the affirmation rabbis bestow on them. Others fear that standing with those who believe in Jewish evangelism might jeopardize their friendship with these rabbis. Many simply don't think through the implications or realize that those they are endorsing oppose Jewish evangelism. In any case, the cause of Christ among the Jewish people is hurt.
>
> You can find examples of good Christians endorsing people who oppose our efforts on the web site of Rabbi Yechiel Eckstein. As director of the International Fellowship of Christians and Jews, Eckstein has diverted tens of millions of dollars in mission giving to his non-missionary efforts. Yet Lloyd Ogilvie, . . . Jerry Falwell, Pat Robertson and Pat Boone as well as the late Bill Bright are all listed on his site with quotes that sing the rabbi's praises. The quotes may not reflect their knowledge of Eckstein's anti-evangelism stance, or even portray their sentiments today, but they are there just the same. Many lay Christians depend on such leaders to help determine if a cause is "kosher." No wonder evangelicals are duped into supporting Rabbi Eckstein.[6]

Unknown to the many evangelical Christians who support Eckstein, his organization does not directly disburse funds to indigent Jews or to Jews wishing to immigrate to Israel. Instead he gives funds raised to other Jewish organizations who then do the acts of charity in their own name. Among the organizations that are recipients of funds are Colel

Chabad, a humanitarian organization related to the Lubavitcher Hasidim, an ultra-Orthodox group that is active not only in humanitarian projects, but in anti-missionary work as well. One can be sure that any Jewish recipient of aid from such an organization who speaks favorably about Jesus or relates an encounter with a Christian missionary will be quickly talked out of considering Jesus.[7] It is significant that Christians sometimes mistake Rabbi Eckstein's organization for a Christian one. At Jews for Jesus, many of us have met at least one person who thought they were supporting a work like Jews for Jesus because they were already supporting the IFCJ. Furthermore, they were unaware that Eckstein was a rabbi and not a Christian evangelist! Some of the endorsements by Christian leaders have contributed to this confusion, as they refer to Eckstein as "brother" or "man of God" or proudly announce that he has spoken in their pulpit.[8]

We commend Christians who want to join in supporting the Jewish people, and we don't intend to tell Christians which causes they should and should not support. Nevertheless, it seems to us that Rabbi Eckstein is deliberately seeking to blur lines, with the effect that many evangelical Christians are persuaded that he is one of them.

Bridges for Peace

Headed by Clarence H. Wagner, this organization seeks to encourage among Christians a love for Israel and a concern for the Jewish people. Their publications include material on the Jewish background of the gospel and have also included strong statements in support of Israel and against replacement theology (the doctrine that the Church has replaced Israel in God's plan).

Bridges for Peace is evangelical in its leadership. Its goals are listed on its web site:

We are committed to the following goals:
- To encourage meaningful and supportive relationships between Christians and Jews in Israel and around the world.
- To educate and equip Christians to identify with Israel, the Jewish people, and the biblical/Hebraic foundations of our Christian faith.
- To bless Israel and the Jewish people in Israel and worldwide, through practical assistance, volunteer service, and prayer.
- To communicate Christian perspectives to the attention of Israeli leaders and the Jewish community-at-large.
- To counter Anti-Semitism worldwide and support Israel's divine God-given right to exist in her God-given land.[9]

All this is commendable, yet it should be pointed out that Bridges for Peace does not include sharing the gospel among the ways one should show love to Jewish people. A perusal of some of their printed materials suggests that they do believe that Jesus is the way of salvation and hints at the fact that some day "all Israel will be saved" (Romans 11:26), yet for now the calling of the Church is only to "bless" and "love" Israel. Anecdotal accounts suggest that Christians visiting Israel under the auspices of Bridges for Peace are encouraged *not* to share their faith.[10] It is noteworthy that Rabbi Eckstein's book mentioned above is listed on the Bridges for Peace recommended reading list.[11]

The International Christian Embassy Jerusalem

Formed in 1980, the ICEJ originated as a counterpoint to a widespread lack of support for Israel as evidenced by the refusal of a number of countries to have their embassies in Jerusalem. The ICEJ attempted to express Christian support and love for the state of Israel "as an evangelical Christian response to the need to comfort Zion according to the command of Scripture found in Isaiah 40:1-2."[12]

However, the organization does not embrace evangelism.[13]
Their website explains their goals in these terms:

> The International Christian Embassy Jerusalem is a
> worldwide, non-profit ministry with a prophetic calling to
> be a source of comfort to Israel and the Jewish people. The
> Bible is clear about the attitude Christians should have
> towards the Jews. Genesis 12:3 says we should "bless
> them." Isaiah 40:1 commands us to "comfort them." Psalm
> 122:6 says we should "pray for the peace of Jerusalem."
> Romans 11:31 tells us to "show them mercy."[14]

In 1990, the Israel branch of the Lausanne Consultation on
Jewish Evangelism issued a statement that included this remark:

> We commend those Christians who are reaching out to
> Israel by humanitarian labors of love and concern.
> However, history cannot excuse the church from its duty to
> preach the Gospel to Israel, nor can Israel be comforted
> truly apart from her Messiah. No good deeds can atone for
> the past, nor may we replace the finished atoning work of
> Messiah with expressions of our love.[15]

Acts of social and personal care are to be welcomed. As
Baruch Maoz, an Israeli Jewish-Christian pastor who authored
the above statement, said elsewhere in the same journal, "Jews
have never suffered from an overdose of Christian affection."
At the same time, the retreat of gospel proclamation to a back
issue or side issue is cause for concern in organizations that
claim to represent the love of Christians for Jews.

Exobus

Founded in 1991, Exobus describes itself as "an international,
prophetic and practical ministry."[16] Headed up by Phil Hunter,

who is the managing director of Good News Travels, a Christian coach company based in England, Exobus raises funds to bring Jewish people to Israel from Russia and Ukraine. They see this as their way to fulfill "the call of God on Jews to return home [meaning the land of Israel]." The coaches (buses) transport Jews from Russia to Poland and then they are carried by other transport to Israel. Like the above groups, Exobus doesn't engage in or specifically encourage Jewish evangelism. While clearly expressing faith in Jesus and the need for worldwide spiritual revival, Exobus seems to believe that the Jewish people need first to return to the Land of Israel in unbelief, after which God will spiritually revive the nation. No mention is made of a present need for Jewish people to hear about Jesus.[17]

CONCLUSION

We live in a time when anti-Semitism seems to be on the rise, particularly in Europe and in many Islamic lands. The current generation has no firsthand recollection of the Holocaust or the rise of the State of Israel. The voices of those who can speak of personal experiences in the Holocaust are becoming fewer and fewer, and propaganda often preempts rational discussion of Israel's right to exist.

In this climate any expression of love, care and concern for the Jewish people is to be encouraged. That is why the modern philo-Semitic agencies pose a dilemma. On one hand, they undoubtedly help Jewish people. Who can argue with praying for Israel, providing material support for immigrants to Israel or encouraging understanding of the State of Israel?

Yet if the gospel is never spoken of by organizations operating under the banner of evangelicalism, misimpression is inevitable— among both Jewish people and evangelical Christians. One might think that as far as Jewish people are concerned, Christianity requires no more than mutual understanding and social concern.

It is difficult to pin down the reasons for this neglect of evangelism. Do these agencies consider evangelism to be necessary, but best done by others? Do they hold to something akin to a two-covenant theology? Do they believe that it is, so to speak, God's job to bring Israel to faith in Jesus while it is the Church's job to only "bless" Israel? Baruch Maoz's comment concerning the International Christian Embassy is apropos:

> It is readily acknowledged that not all evangelical bodies must be involved in evangelism. Indeed, some such bodies definitely should not. Their callings are different, and should be conducted accordingly. There would be no difficulty if the Embassy issued a statement to the effect that, while it believed in the necessity of evangelism *per se*, it did not itself engage in such activity. But the Embassy's repeated hedging on this issue gives credence to the growing conviction of some that the Embassy believes political and economic support in the name of Christ are all that is needed, and that evangelism is, at best, peripheral.[18]

Previous generations embraced liberalism to the extent that the basics of the gospel were replaced with the "social gospel." Will this generation purposely embrace a political and social love for Jewish people without proclaiming Him who is our only political, social and spiritual hope? One is reminded of Jesus' saying that certain things should be done without neglecting the others (Matthew 23:23).

Jews for Jesus encourages people to consider practical ways of expressing love to Jewish people they know. But we also consider sharing the gospel with a Jewish person the ultimate reflection of care and concern, even though it often involves risking relationships.

We would never want to dictate to anyone where their support should go. But at least let those who support the philo-Semitic organizations understand who and what they are supporting, especially when it comes to the question of the most loving thing you can do for a Jewish person—that is, proclaiming the gospel. Jews for Jesus is in touch with forthright Christian relief efforts to the Jewish poor in Israel and elsewhere, and will supply such information upon request.

FURTHER READING

On Rabbi Yechiel Eckstein:
   The War on Jewish Evangelism
   http://files.jewsforjesus.org/pdf/other/war_on_je.pdf

   Moishe Rosen concerning "On Wings of Eagles"
   http://www.jewsforjesus.org/publications/newsletter/1997
   _03/sayings

   Moishe's Musings on Lifestyle Evangelism
   http://www.jewsforjesus.org/publications/newsletter/2000
   _11/moishesmusings

On Philo-Semitic Organizations:
   Goldberg, Louis, "Historical and Political Factors in the Twentieth Century Affecting the Identity of Israel." In *Israel: The Land and the People: An Evangelical Affirmation of God's Promises*, edited by H. Wayne House. Grand Rapids, MI: Kregel Publications, 1998.

   Skarsaune, Oskar, "The Neglected Story of Christian Philo-Semitism in Antiquity and the Early Middle Ages," *Mishkan: A Theological Forum on the Gospel and the Jewish People*, vol. 21, 1994, 40-51.

   Mishkan: A Theological Forum on Jewish Evangelism 12, 1990, issue including material on the Christian Embassy. http://www.caspari.com/mishkan/contents/contents11.html#12

On loving the Jewish people:

Bärend, Irmhild, "Why I, a German, Love the Jewish People." *ISSUES* 13:7. http://www.jewsforjesus.org/publications/issues/13_7/whyi lovethejews

Damato, Catherine, "Why I, a Gentile, Love the Jewish People." *ISSUES* 11:1. http://www.jewsforjesus.org/publications/issues/11_1/whyi lovethejews

Notes

1. See Oskar Skarsaune, "The Neglected Story of Christian Philo-Semitism in Antiquity and the Early Middle Ages," *Mishkan: A Theological Forum on the Gospel and the Jewish People* 21 (1994): 40-51. Skarsaune also references scholars John Gager and Stephen Wilson in support.

2. On Two-Covenant theology see *Mishkan:* 11 (1989). The entire issue was given over to this subject.

3. http://www.ifcj.org/site/PageServer?pagename=programs_faq

4. Eckstein, Yechiel. *What Christians Should Know About Jews and Judaism* (Waco: Word, 1984), p. 287.

5. Samuelson, Francine K. "Messianic Judaism: Church, Denomination, Sect, or Cult?," *Journal of Ecumenical Studies* 37:2 (Spring 2000), p. 174, citing *What Christians Should Know*, pp. 297-298; and "Joan Watson, telephone conversation with author, September 15, 1998."

6. Brickner, David, "The War on Jewish Evangelism," 2003, online as a PDF at: http://files.jewsforjesus.org/pdf/other/war_on_je.pdf. A website that brings together many relevant quotes by Eckstein and his supporters can be found at: http://www.myfortress.org/RabbiYechielEckstein.html

7. For a complete list of 2003 recipients of IFJC's aid, see their annual report available at: http://www.ifcj.org/site/PageServer?pagename=whoweare_annualreport

8. http://www.ifcj.org/site/PageServer?pagename=endorsements and http://www.myfortress.org/RabbiYechielEckstein.html

9. http://www.bridgesforpeace.com/h2n.php?fn=whoarewe.html

10. Goldberg, Louis. "Historical and Political Factors in the Twentieth Century Affecting the Identity of Israel," pp. 113-141 in *Israel, the Land and the People: An Evangelical Affirmation of God's Promises*, ed. H. Wayne House (Grand Rapids: Kregel, 1998), p. 131.

11. http://www.bridgesforpeace.com/h2n.php?fn=research.html# JEWISH-CHRISTIAN%20UNDERSTANDING

12. http://www.icej.org/

13. Goldberg, "Historical Factors," pp. 131-32.

14. http://www.icej.org/comfort/index.html

15. "A Statement on Christian Zionism," *Mishkan* 12 (1990), p. 6.

16. http://www.exobus.org

17. http://www.exobus.org/featuresstory.asp?id=286&section=reg3

18. Maoz, Baruch. "The Christian Embassy in Jerusalem," *Mishkan* 12 (1990), pp. 2-3.

Part Two

Movements Within the Movement

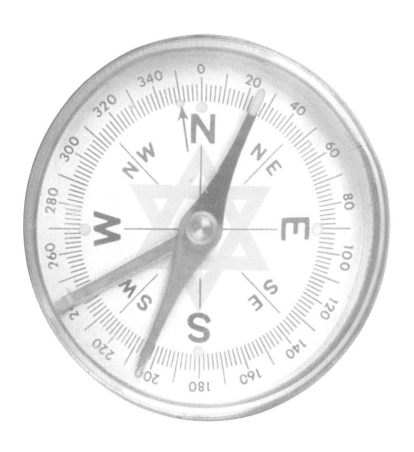

Chapter One
Questioning the Jewishness
of Christian Theology

INTRODUCTION

In an effort to "restore" or emphasize the Jewishness of the gospel, a teaching has surfaced among some in the Messianic movement who maintain that the cardinal doctrines of Christianity such as the Incarnation and the Trinity are pagan in origin, and that observances such as Christmas and Easter are based in paganism and are to be rejected as unbiblical or "unJewish."

The first thing to keep in mind is that the gospel is cross-cultural, and this means that Jewish forms of worship and lifestyle are not mandatory for the Church at large. Jewish believers may enjoy expressing their faith in Jewish terms by, for instance, celebrating the Passover and holding a seder in their home or displaying Jewish art. Such practices should be encouraged. But these activities are not incumbent on Korean, Malaysian or Nigerian Christians.

The charge of paganism, though, pertains less to what Christians should do or believe; rather, it seeks to tell Christians what they should *not* do or believe. And charges of paganism might not be thorough-going; some who question the appropriateness of celebrating Christmas might not challenge the doctrines of the Incarnation or the Trinity; they may be quite orthodox in that regard. This chapter looks at the various allegations of paganism in Christian thought and practice.

RESPONDING TO THE CHARGES OF
PAGANISM OF CHRISTIAN PRACTICES

First, let's consider the charge that believers shouldn't observe

Christmas and Easter because they were pagan in origin. There are several problems with this approach.

One problem has to do with the use of symbols. Symbols are a language and, as with any language, their meaning depends on usage, not origins. God's people have long used pagan or secular symbols and institutions with new, sanctified meanings. For example, in the Old Testament, sanctuaries, temples, priests and sacrifices existed among the pagan nations long before Israel was formed. God, however, took those institutions and turned them into sanctified symbols that reflected who He was and how He wanted His people to live.

In the New Testament, Jesus took post-biblical customs such as the four cups of wine at Passover and the water-drawing ceremonies of Sukkot and invested them with new meaning concerning Himself (or, as some might phrase it, He explained their old meaning with application to Himself). In more recent history, Johann Sebastian Bach was known to take secular drinking songs and convert them into church hymns to the glory of God.

The date on which Christmas is now celebrated, December 25, did indeed coincide with a pagan holiday. It is quite possible, however, that the date was deliberately adopted by the Church in order to sanctify the day, invest it with new meaning and perhaps even reach out evangelistically. The same holds true for Easter, whose name derives from the Saxon goddess Eostre, but which may have been intended to be a Christian replacement for a pagan celebration rather than an accommodation to one. But again, the origins are not as important as the present meaning associated with the holiday.

Further, once you say that you can't celebrate Christmas or Easter because of their pagan origins, where do you stop? The seven days of the week are, in the English language, named for pagan Norse gods. To be consistent, those who advocate abandoning Christmas or Easter on the grounds of pagan origins should stop calling the days of the week by their common names. The planets are likewise named after Roman gods and common words like "odyssey" have their origins in non-Christian, pagan literature. But of course none of these things pays homage to Greek or Norse gods in daily usage. Origins do not determine meaning.

One pastor and historian sums it up this way:

> The regular worship of the church in the early centuries has been closely studied by scholars. Its changing forms have been carefully documented. Such changes are no cause for alarm, in themselves. The Passover celebrated by Jesus embraced a traditional course of four wine cups which was not specified in the Law. Furthermore, Jesus appears to have taken part in the Feast of Dedication (Hannukah), referred to in John 10:22f, which was an inter-testamental celebration recalling the days of the Maccabees. These traditions were acceptable because [they were] not alien to what the Law *did* require. This fact is helpful when considering customs in worship and Christian observance (such as Christmas), which are not commanded in Scripture.[1] [emphasis in the original]

Saying a particular worship form or holiday isn't culturally Jewish is one thing, though one can argue that celebrating the Messiah's birth or resurrection is in fact Jewish. But to go further and call them unbiblical is quite another.

RESPONDING TO THE CHARGES OF PAGANISM OF CHRISTIAN DOCTRINES

Claims that Christian concepts such as the Incarnation and the Trinity are of pagan origin are not new, nor are they specifically

Jewish assertions. In the context of this book, it should be noted that some who make these claims are at times identified as being part of the Messianic movement—but their theology, insofar as they reject the Incarnation and the Trinity, is not evangelical. In fact, in that regard their thinking is quite similar to that of anti-missionaries and many secular scholars.

There are resources available that explain how these doctrines did not originate in paganism; some of them are listed at the end of this chapter. But few accounts go further and demonstrate that these doctrines are *distinctly Jewish*.

The Doctrine of the Incarnation

One scholar who has done much work in this area is Oskar Skarsaune, professor of church history at the Norwegian Lutheran School of Theology in Oslo, Norway.

In his book, *In the Shadow of the Temple*,[2] Skarsaune observes, "Jewish scholars in antiquity, the Middle Ages and modern times have almost unanimously claimed that the idea that Jesus is the incarnate Word of God is un-Jewish, a product of Christianity's transplantation from a Jewish milieu to a Gentile-Hellenistic milieu." (And, we add, not just mainstream Jewish scholars, but as indicated above, some who might be considered part of the Messianic movement also hold this view.) However, the evidence substantiates the opposite conclusion, as Skarsaune goes on to show:

> Let us begin with an observation on the typical Hellenistic reaction to the dogma of the incarnate Son of God. [Orthodox Jewish scholar Pinchas] Lapide would have us believe that this was something Gentile Hellenists would really appreciate, something they craved for, something

they would embrace enthusiastically. But we have several authentic reports on the Gentile Hellenistic reaction, and it does not correspond to this picture at all. The available evidence shows, on the contrary, that most Hellenists reacted with disgust and contempt at the very idea of a divine incarnation, and with charges of blasphemy when they heard that the incarnate Son of God had suffered the uttermost shame of crucifixion.[3]

Skarsaune traces the roots of the doctrine of the Incarnation to the Jewish concept of the Wisdom of God in the Old Testament and inter-testamental periods.[4] And he gives us a rather startling quote from Pinchas Lapide:

> I used to think that becoming incarnate was impossible to God. But recently I have come to the conclusion that it is un-Jewish to say that this is something the God of the Bible cannot do, that he cannot come that close. I have had second thoughts about the incarnation.[5]

The Doctrine of the Trinity

Similarly, research on the doctrine of the Trinity shows its essentially Jewish character. A case in point is the work of Larry W. Hurtado. Hurtado is professor of New Testament Language, Literature and Theology at the University of Edinburgh's School of Divinity and director of the Centre for the Study of Christian Origins. Hurtado has written extensively on the early Christian understanding that Jesus was divine. For the full argument, interested readers can refer to his books in the section on further reading. The following, however, summarizes his conclusions:

> Devotion to Jesus as divine erupted suddenly and quickly, not gradually and late, among first-century circles of followers. More specifically, the origins lie in Jewish

Christian circles of the earliest years. Only a certain wishful thinking continues to attribute the reverence of Jesus as divine decisively to the influence of pagan religion and the influx of Gentile converts, characterizing it as developing late and incrementally.[6]

In other words, the doctrine of the deity of Jesus is not some fourth century development foisted on the Church by Gentile believers. There is no "non-divine Jesus" in first-century Christianity that needs to be "restored" in the name of Jewishness. It is true that the doctrine did not take the form in which we know it for a few centuries after Jesus' ministry.

> But the doctrinal problem they [church councils] worked on was not of their making. It was forced upon them by the earnest convictions and devotional practices of believers from the earliest observable years of the Christian movement.[7]

Hurtado, in his wide-ranging study, traces the early devotion to Jesus as a "variant" of exclusive Jewish monotheism, in sharp contrast to typical pagan ideas of "apotheosis" (the transformation of a human being into a god). In other words, we are dealing with a case where God becomes man, not where man becomes divine. Interestingly, he quotes first-century Jewish writer Philo, responding to the emperor Gaius Caligula's claim to be divine: "Sooner could God change into a man than a man into God." Hurtado remarks that this quotation is illustrative of the Jewish attitudes of the time.[8]

CONCLUSION

In the end, study of Scripture and the history of theological ideas shows the Jewishness of Christian doctrine, as well as the propriety of sanctifying non-Christian practices to the service of God.

Some in the Messianic movement use the history of anti-Semitism within the Church as a justification for avoiding the contributions made by the largely non-Jewish Church in the centuries after Christ. But those who wish to bypass, neglect, or replace the fruit of 2,000 years of theology fail to appreciate that God has worked within the Church in spite of its failings. Furthermore, the inclusion of Gentiles within the people of God was part of God's purposes since He proclaimed in Genesis 12:1-3 that through Abraham, the entire world would be blessed. If God intended Gentiles to become part of God's people, how then can we neglect their contributions or stereotype them as pagan? Those who neglect the fruit of Gentile theologians are guilty of the very same thing as those they accuse of neglecting Jewish thought.

FURTHER READING

Hurtado, Larry W., *Lord Jesus Christ: Devotion to Jesus in Earliest Christianity*. Grand Rapids and Cambridge: Eerdmans, 2003.

Nash, Ronald H., *The Gospel and the Greeks: Did the New Testament Borrow from Pagan Thought?* P & R Publishing; 2nd ed., 2003.

Skarsaune, Oskar, *In the Shadow of the Temple: Jewish Influences on Early Christianity*. Downers Grove: InterVarsity Press, 2002.

Skarsaune, Oskar, *Incarnation: Myth or Fact*. Concordia Publishing House, 1991.

Davies, W. D., *Paul and Rabbinic Judaism: Some Rabbinic Elements in Pauline Theology*. Fortress Press, 4th edition, 1980. Originally published 1948.

Nash, Ronald, "Was the New Testament Influenced by Pagan Religions?"

http://www.iclnet.org/pub/resources/text/cri/
cri-jrnl/web/crj0169a.txt

Nash, Ronald. "Was the New Testament Influenced by Pagan Philosophy?"
http://www.iclnet.org/pub/resources/text/cri/cri-jrnl/web/crj0163a.html

Miller, Glenn. "Was Jesus Christ just a CopyCat Savior Myth?"
http://www.christian-thinktank.com/copycat.html

Miller, Glenn. "Were the New Testament authors influenced by pagan legends?"
http://www.christian-thinktank.com/copycat2.html

Notes

1. Jackson, Jeremy C., *No Other Foundation: The Church Through Twenty Centuries* (Westchester, IL: Cornerstone Books, 1980), p. 53.
2. Skarsaune, Oskar. *In the Shadow of the Temple: Jewish Influences on Early Christianity*. Downers Grove: InterVarsity Press, 2002.
3. Ibid., p. 323.
4. See also his earlier book, *Incarnation: Myth or Fact* (Concordia Publishing House, 1991).
5. Skarsaune, *In the Shadow*, pp. 335-36, citing "Norwegian television, April 1978. There seems to be no taped copy of this interview preserved by Norwegian Broadcasting, but Lapide's words made such an impression upon me that they stuck in my mind."
6. Hurtado, Larry W., *Lord Jesus Christ: Devotion to Jesus in Earliest Christianity*. Grand Rapids and Cambridge: Eerdmans, 2003, p. 650.
7. Ibid., p. 651.
8. Ibid., pp. 91-92, citing Philo, *Embassy to Gaius,* 118.

Chapter Two
About "Torah Observance"

INTRODUCTION

Among those groups that are sometimes considered part of the Messianic movement are those organizations and congregations that call themselves "Torah-observant" or emphasize obedience to the Law of Moses by another term. As a random sampling, such groups may include educational organizations, such as the First Fruits of Zion, individual congregations, such as Petah Tikvah in Rochester, New York or associations such as the Observant Messianic Jewish Rabbinical Association.[1] These groups can vary from the theologically orthodox regarding the person of Christ and the Trinity, to theologically aberrant. Essentially, these groups present themselves as following the Old Testament Law of Moses, thereby living a life they believe more closely resembles that of first-century followers of Jesus, or is more in keeping with God's will for today.

LOOKING AT THE LAW

Martin Luther once observed that no sooner does someone fall off a horse on the right side, than they get back on and proceed to fall off on the left side. The Torah-observant groups are in part a reaction against negative views of the Law found in some Christian circles. It is the unfortunate case that in much of evangelical Christianity the Old Testament is hardly taught, rarely preached on and little understood by the average congregant. Where the Law is mentioned, it is often portrayed as merely a burden from which Christians are now free.

The biblical picture of the Law is quite different. The Law in the Old Testament is spoken of as a gift from God, a guide to life, something to be cherished and enjoyed, as well as something to be obeyed under penalty of disobedience. It is intimately bound up with the covenant wherein God graciously reiterated His relationship with His people.

In the New Testament, the Apostle Paul reminds us that the Law is good.[2] The idea of obedience is continually highlighted, from the Sermon on the Mount to Jesus' words in John's Gospel[3] and in the Epistles.[4] In fact, nine of the Ten Commandments are explicitly reinforced in the New Testament.

The Law itself is not bad; it is sin, the misuse of the Law, and the way that human traditions can end up supplanting the Law, that are bad. The principles of the Law, especially the Ten Commandments, have become the bedrock of Western civilization and of the Church itself—even those churches that portray the Law negatively.

Having said this, the Christian church has universally recognized that the Law of Moses is not meant to be kept as a body of law by Christians today.[5] The Law of Moses was part of a covenant that God made with Israel at a particular time and in a particular place. With the coming of Christ, the New Covenant prophesied by Jeremiah has come into effect and we are no longer under the Old Covenant.

The fact is that for the past two thousand years it has been impossible to observe all the commandments of the Law of Moses because so many of them depend on the existence of a Temple, a priesthood, animal sacrifices and living as a theocratic nation within the Land of Israel. Orthodox Judaism recognizes this, and when the Temple was destroyed in A.D. 70, Judaism was reconstructed as a religion without a Temple or a priesthood, a religion dependent on the authority and decisions of the rabbis. Reform Judaism, a recent movement of the past 250 years, views the Law as often antiquated and outdated, but useful as a reminder of our history, a symbol of our people and a source of ethics.

It is, however, equally important to note that the recognition that we are not intended to keep the Law of Moses today does not mean that Christians believe in lawlessness! The specific commands of the Law of Moses each reflected something of the nature of God, and behind each commandment is a principle. Those principles, reflecting God Himself, are still incumbent on all Christians today. See more on this point in the following section.

A RESPONSE TO TORAH-OBSERVANT GROUPS

In evaluating the "Torah-observant" groups within the Messianic movement, there are several things worth considering. To be sure, the exact nature and function of the Law of Moses are debated among Christians, but with an understanding that the Church, including both Jewish and Gentile members, is not mandated to keep the entire Law of Moses. The following then, is not intended as a final word by any means (as if it were possible in just a few paragraphs!), but is meant to give food for thought, and hopefully pause to those who would rush into attempting to observe the Law of Moses today.

1. It is no longer possible to keep all 613 (if we accept the traditional rabbinic enumeration) laws because we no longer have a Temple, or a priesthood, or live as a theocracy in the Land of Israel. Because of this, the Torah-observant groups end up being extremely selective in their "law-observance." For the most part, the emphasis is on holy days—Sabbaths and festivals—with perhaps some attention given to other parts of the Law. In essence, these are not so much Torah-observant as festival-observant groups. And since the Temple and

priesthood are gone and a majority of Jews live in the diaspora (outside the land of Israel), even the festivals, for instance, must be observed differently than they were in biblical times. Perhaps without their realizing it, Torah-observant groups must either depend on rabbinic tradition, which is distinctly post-biblical, or must construct their own traditions. For instance, members of such groups do not send their men to appear before the Lord in Jerusalem, as required in the Law of Moses, nor do they offer sacrifices. So there can be no question of this being an authentic, first-century way of observance.

Moreover, among the commandments of the Law are penalties for its violation, including the death penalty in many cases. Torah-observant groups do not apply the death penalty to those who are not Torah-observant. Indeed they cannot, for if they did, they would be subject in modern society to criminal charges in a court of law! We no longer live in a theocracy subject to the penalties of God's Law.

2. One gets the impression that far more than they emphasize faithfulness to Christ, the Torah-observant groups emphasize "Torah-observance" as their distinctive, and in fact imply that they are being more obedient to God, or have a deeper spirituality, than other believers in Jesus. Perhaps they would argue that their obedience to the Torah *is* faithfulness to Christ, but there is a distinct imbalance in their approach. Inadvertently, perhaps, they have created a two-tier system of believers: the more spiritual ones who observe the Law and the less spiritual ones who do not. This is not only unbiblical, but it also separates these groups from the rest of the Body of Christ in an unhealthy way.

3. Since much of the Torah-observant movement is a reaction to negative teaching about the Law, there is likewise a failure on the part of this movement to recognize that large segments of the Church take a very positive view of the Law. This is

particularly true of Reformed and Presbyterian churches, which include a positive emphasis on God's law within their confessional statements, and in their preaching and teaching. What they mean by God's law, however, is not the specific 613 commandments of the Law of Moses—which was part of the Mosaic covenant intended for that time in redemptive history—but the principles that God intends for us and commands us to live by. For many of these churches, those principles are embodied especially in the Ten Commandments, which comprise the standard for all Christian obedience.

4. Actually, the obedience required under the New Covenant is more radical than that under the Old Covenant. For instance, in Deuteronomy 22:8, it is required for one to build a parapet around the roof, a safety feature in a time when the roof functioned as both a living room for entertaining and a bedroom. I doubt that the Torah-observant groups require such parapets. But under the New Covenant, *much more* is required. That particular commandment is an example of how to follow the general rule to love our neighbor and is an outworking of the Sixth Commandment, "You shall not murder." In principle, its application today would range from preserving safety for our family and guests all the way to working for national security or in public policy. The New Covenant broadens and deepens the requirements of the Law of Moses: "For everyone to whom much is given, from him much will be required" (Luke 12:48). To stress obedience to the Law of Moses without stressing the fuller applications of the principles embodied in those laws is to miss the point (Galatians 3:24).

5. The Torah-observant groups justify their position on the basis of selected verses, while ignoring others. Much is made of the term "forever" used in regard to some Old Testament laws, while verses such as Hebrews 8:13, that speak of the first covenant as being "obsolete," are not dealt with. Further,

they ignore what theologians commonly call the "history of redemption," the progress of God's dealings with humankind throughout history. Jesus has indeed brought something new, but the Torah-observant groups minimize the newness that the coming of the Messiah has meant. In addition, they minimize the way much Old Testament Law functioned to distinguish Israel from the nations. While there is indeed distinctiveness to the Jewish people, not all the Old Testament distinctions apply. For example, one can make a good argument that the food laws were intended to symbolize the separation of Israel from the nations. Under the New Covenant, Jewish and Gentile believers in Jesus become one in the Messiah (Ephesians 2:14) in a way not realized under the Mosaic Covenant. As a result, one can build a good case that the mandatory keeping of kosher laws is no longer required for a Jewish believer in Jesus.[6]

6. Many in Torah-observant circles are not Jewish. Thought should be given as to why non-Jews are so eager to observe a law never intended for them, and to the New Testament teaching on the place of the Law of Moses in the lives of Gentile Christians.

CONCLUSION
With Jewish observances, questions arise about whether or not particular observances are proper for a follower of Jesus, and these questions have been debated among Jewish believers. One problem is that it is often hard to separate cultural from religious expressions. For an Orthodox Jew, celebrating Passover is a fulfillment of a divine command, and is done in accordance with the accretions of 2,000 years of rabbinic tradition and rabbinic law. For a Reform or secular Jew, celebrating Passover is often simply an opportunity to enjoy doing something Jewish: having a get-together with the family, going through a few traditions familiar from childhood and sharing a meal. Is Passover then a cultural expression or a religious one? Similar questions arise pertaining to

other aspects of Judaism, because Judaism today is not a monolith when it comes to religious and cultural expression.

Therefore, a word needs to be said about the place of the Law of Moses in the life of a Jewish believer. Some Messianic congregations have a *Sefer Torah*, a scroll of the Law. Many, even if they do not own a *Sefer Torah*, incorporate readings from the Torah that correspond to the passage being read that week in synagogues in their services. Many Jewish believers choose to celebrate the holidays or keep kosher. Usually, though, this is something quite different from the intentions of the Torah-observant groups. For instance, all the above examples might be done to show solidarity with the rest of the Jewish community, to express worship in a Jewish manner, to be a testimony to other Jewish people, or simply as a mark of personal Jewish identity. If done voluntarily, without a belief that one accrues higher favor with God for doing so, there is freedom in Christ to do these things. However, the emphasis of Torah-observant groups is on mandatory law-keeping as an expression of greater obedience to God. So in their case we are dealing with something quite different.

A word also about churches that enjoy such celebrations as Passover: this is also something quite different from the Torah-observant groups. Churches that have an annual Passover Seder generally do so as a teaching and worship tool, with fulfillment in Christ as the focus, and an emphasis on enriching the observance of Communion. In such circumstances, it is not done as part of a mandatory requirement to observe the Law of Moses. As such, this activity should be encouraged.[7]

In summary, if you hear of a group calling themselves "Torah-observant," keep in mind the above responses and remember that it was never the Law, only its misuse, that the New Testament criticizes.

FURTHER READING

Strickland, Wayne G., ed., *Five Views on Law and Gospel.*
Zondervan, 1996. A helpful though challenging read on
different views among evangelical Christians of the place of
the Law of Moses for the Christian.

Wenham, David., "Jesus and the Law: An Exegesis on Matthew
5:17-20." *Mishkan* 8/9, 1988. Available at:
http://www.caspari.com/mishkan

Kaiser, Walter C., Jr. "James' View of the Law." *Mishkan* 8/9, 1988.

ONLINE RESOURCES

Lieske, Bruce J., "Jewish Feasts in Gentile Congregations." *Papers
for August 8-9 from the Lausanne Consultation on Jewish
Evangelism, Fourth International Conference, Zeist Holland,*
1991. 247-51. An example of an approach from a Lutheran pastor
that finds educational and worship value in the Jewish festivals
without advocating them as mandatory, necessary for obedience
to God, or indispensable to Christian growth. Available at:
http://www.jewsforjesus.org/publications/lieske

Shore, Alan M., "The Torah of God: Road Back or Road Block?
A Look at Law in Judaism and Christianity." *ISSUES* 6:2, 1988.
Includes a look at how the Law functions in rabbinic Judaism
and the relationship of Jesus to Torah.
Available at:
http://www.jewsforjesus.org/publications/issues/6_2/torahofgod

Mishkan 4, 1986. Available as a PDF download at:
http://www.caspari.com/mishkan/zips/mishkan04.pdf
Includes "Paul, the Law and the Covenant" by Ray Kearsley
(response by Stephen Notley) and "Jesus, the Kingdom and the
Torah" by Ole Chr. M. Kvarme (response by Ronald H. Lewis).

TORAH OBSERVANT GROUPS MENTIONED ABOVE

First Fruits of Zion
www.ffoz.org

Petah Tikvah
http://www.petahtikvah.com

Observant Messianic Jewish Rabbinical Association
http://www.omjra.org

Notes

1. See for instance the listing at:
http://www.omjra.org/Members.html
2. Romans 7:12, 16.
3. "If you love me, you will obey what I command" (John 14:15).
4. For instance: "But the man who looks intently into the perfect law that gives freedom, and continues to do this, not forgetting what he has heard, but doing it—he will be blessed in what he does" (James 1:25); "If you really keep the royal law found in Scripture, "Love your neighbor as yourself," you are doing right" (James 2:8); "What good is it, my brothers, if a man claims to have faith but has no deeds? Can such faith save him?" (James 2:14).
5. Many divide the Law into civil, ceremonial and moral laws. Whether those are valid distinctions is another matter, but it is instructive that no one insists that we need to keep them all. Most Christians who view the Law along those three divisions accept an ongoing validity to the moral law, particularly as embodied in the Ten Commandments. A minority view is that of Theonomists, who believe that the civil law with its penalties should continue to function in some way today.
6. For a good discussion of the laws of kosher food in Leviticus, see Wenham, Gordon J., *The Book of Leviticus* (New International Commentary on the Old Testament; Eerdmans, 1979).
7. See Lieske, Bruce J., "Jewish Feasts in Gentile Congregations," at http://www.jewsforjesus.org/publications/lieske/

Chapter Three
The Hebrew Roots Movement

INTRODUCTION

The Hebrew Roots movement, sometimes also called the Hebraic Roots or Jewish Roots movement, is one indicator of an increased interest on the part of Christians in exploring the Jewishness of their faith. One definition, from within this movement, is this:

> The Hebrew Roots movement is composed of a diverse variety of believers and ministries, united in the conviction that our understanding of the New Testament, our relationship with our Savior, and the mission of the Church can all be enhanced by a greater knowledge of the Jewish background of Christianity.[1]

So far so good. It turns out, however, that a great deal is encompassed in the word "diverse" in the above definition. A more specific description might go like this: The Hebrew Roots movement is a movement of organizations, closely networked, that hold in common an emphasis on studying, participating in, or "restoring" the Jewishness of Christianity through some or all of the following: studying the Bible in its Jewish context; observing the Torah; keeping the Sabbath and festivals;[2] avoiding the alleged "paganism" of Christianity; affirming the existence of original Hebrew language gospels and denigrating the Greek text.

Some organizations that are part of this movement emphasize *study*; some add *practice*, especially of the Old Testament festivals; others are interested in what they term *restoration*— getting the Church back to what they understand to be the "original" Jewishness of the Christian faith.

A BIT OF BACKGROUND

So what sets the Hebrew Roots movement apart? After all, most Jewish missions and Messianic congregations want to teach their constituency something about the Jewishness of the gospel (study); many hold demonstrations of the Jewish holidays, or have full celebrations of them (practice); and most would like to see the church recognize its Jewish roots. As will become apparent below, the Hebrew Roots movement often goes beyond an appreciation of Christianity's Jewishness to more controversial areas.

It is difficult to trace a history of the Hebrew Roots movement, which seems to have mushroomed since the advent of the Internet. Undoubtedly, several influences have been at work in its growth. One is the increasing appreciation for the Jewishness of Christianity, both among Jewish and Christian scholars. This interest has been a hallmark of some Jewish scholarship since the Enlightenment, but has been given added impetus by the post-Holocaust move away from evangelism toward dialogue (hence, the desire to find commonality in the Jewishness of Jesus), the rise of the State of Israel (encouraging archaeological explorations, including those related to Christianity), and the discovery of the Dead Sea Scrolls (further highlighting the Jewish background of the New Testament).

To that mix, add the increasing appreciation for Jesus' Jewishness among evangelical Christians. Some Jewish believers of past generations complained about anti-Semitism in the churches and a refusal to allow Jewish believers the freedom to express their faith in a Jewish way. In today's evangelical churches, the response to hearing about Jews who come to faith is likely to be positive, and churches often explore the Jewish background of their faith by, for instance, holding an annual Passover Seder. Many Christians, too, have become ardent supporters of the modern State of Israel. With this background, it is not hard to see how the Hebrew Roots movement has grown.[3]

Geographically, many Hebrew Roots organizations are based in the Midwest and South (Ohio, Oklahoma, Texas, Arkansas, etc.), in areas where there are relatively few Jews.

Despite the fact that one website cites interest in Jewish evangelism as a factor behind the rise of the Hebrew Roots movement, that interest is not plainly seen in most of the ministries involved. Rather, their emphasis is on learning and doing Jewish things. Some, such as John Garr's Restoration Foundation, explicitly promote Jewish-Christian dialogue, with no mention of evangelism.

RESPONDING TO HEBREW ROOTS GROUPS

Many Christians would be enriched to rediscover the Jewishness of Jesus. For this reason, it is regrettable that words of caution need to be said in regard to the Hebrew Roots movement. These warnings fit into two categories: first, regarding the indiscriminate networking and linking among the organizations; second, regarding the actual teachings of some of the organizations.

Networking and Linking

The average evangelical Christian who approaches a website such as www.hebroots.org may think that all the organizations and resources listed are evangelical in orientation, especially if his or her first contact with the movement came via an evangelical Hebrew Roots ministry. But the networking among Hebrew Roots groups is often without regard for orthodoxy. For example, the Restoration Foundation links to The Friends of Israel Gospel Ministry (an evangelical mission to Jews), Netivyah (an evangelical teaching ministry in Israel),

a host of Hebrew Roots organizations (of varying
perspectives) and news reports produced by Jerusalem Bible
College (an evangelical Bible college in Israel).Another listing
of "Hebrew/Jewish Roots Christian Ministries" includes groups
as disparate as First Fruits of Zion (a Torah-observant group),
Marvin Wilson (an evangelical Christian college professor),
Bridges for Peace (a non-evangelistic "love Israel"
organization), a homeschooling site, and the International
Fellowship of Christians and Jews and its ministry On Wings
of Eagles (whose director, Rabbi Yechiel Eckstein, is an
adamant opponent of Jewish evangelism and Messianic Jews).
What do all these have in common? They all merely have
something to do with Jews and Jesus.

It's not that Christians should only be exposed to evangelical
teachings.The concern is that indiscriminate networking may
give the impression that all such organizations are evangelical
teaching ministries, sound in doctrine and practice—when in
fact the converse is sometimes the case.

Specific Teachings and Practices
It is difficult to characterize the Hebrew Roots movement
as holding to any one set of doctrines. Some organizations
offer statements of faith that are evangelical concerning
the doctrines of Christ and of salvation, although they add
points that most Christians would consider unbiblical
concerning the need to keep the Law of Moses or the
Jewish festivals. Several espouse the idiosyncratic (but
influential) "Two-House Theory," which asserts that the
Church is the lost tribe of Ephraim, the idea being that
many or all Gentile Christians are descendants of the so-
called "Ten Lost Tribes" (see Chapter 2.4). In fact, there is
a good amount of affiliation and overlap between many
Hebrew Roots and Two-House organizations. For instance,
Edward Chumney, who has written in support of the Two-

House theory, is news director for "Restore!" a magazine published by the Restoration Foundation. Similarly, the Hebrew Roots of Christianity Global Network website links to materials on the Two-House theory.

One teaching institution that is part of the Hebrew Roots movement is the American Institute of Middle Eastern Studies (formerly called the Arkansas Institute of Holy Land Studies), headed by Ron Moseley. Faculty members include Roy Blizzard, Marvin Wilson and Brad Young. Not all are evangelical. To be sure, there are many things one can learn from non-evangelicals or non-believers in an academic setting. What is disconcerting is not that the faculty come from a variety of theological viewpoints, but that in a ministry that is promulgated to evangelical Christians, and suggests that it is Christian in basis, there is no mention of its faculty's theological positions. Marvin Wilson is an evangelical scholar at Gordon College and Brad Young teaches at Oral Roberts University. On the other hand, Roy Blizzard's view of the Trinity is not evangelical: "And now we have the Father, Son, and Holy Spirit. That idea is a very late development in Christian theology. As a matter of fact, it's not developed to any degree until the fourth century. When it is put forth by the church, they argue over it for about 40 years before it is finally adopted. The man who proposed it initially was banished eight times for heresy. It's not Hebrew."[4] But who would know that from the website?

Having said this, it's time to delve further into the three areas related to the Hebrew Roots movement mentioned above: study, practice and "restoration."

Study
The study of the Jewishness of the Christian faith is to be encouraged. Unfortunately, the way in which the Jewishness of Christianity is presented in much of the Hebrew Roots

movement does not always accurately reflect what most
scholars believe. For instance, one organization within this
network is HaKesher, the ministry of Robert Lindsay. Lindsay is
one of the scholars who helped promulgate the "original
Hebrew gospels" view, which states that the gospels as we have
them in Greek are only translations of documents originally
written in Hebrew.

In *Mishkan* 17-18 (1992/1993), respected Jewish Christian
apologist Michael L. Brown responded to this view of the New
Testament with a "discommendation" of the book
Understanding the Difficult Words of Jesus by Blizzard and
Bivin, and with a stern word of warning concerning the
overall approach of the Jerusalem School of Synoptic Research
to biblical reliability. The "original Hebrew" view of the
gospels is not accepted by most scholars, not because of anti-
Jewish bias, but because in their view the evidence does not
support it. Furthermore, these scholars are quick to point out
that if the "original Hebrew" hypothesis is believed, then the
inerrancy of Scripture must be questioned.

On the same topic of study and learning, the Hebrew Roots
movement appears to be rather ingrown. While the work of
those involved is given continual prominence, in some of the
ministries it is rarely suggested that one can learn much about
the Jewishness of Christianity from mainstream Christian
sources. The fact is that any good commentary will give Jewish
backgrounds and explanations; whole series of books have
been written on the Jewish (and Greek/Roman) backgrounds
to the New Testament. Gentile scholars such as W. D. Davies
and Jewish ones such as David Daube have written extensively
on the Jewishness of Jesus. Periodicals like *Mishkan: A
Theological Forum on Jewish Evangelism* have been
produced for some twenty years, focusing on the Jewishness of
Jesus. But one hears hardly a word about any of this from

many in the Hebrew Roots movement. It is almost as if they alone have rediscovered the Jewishness of the gospel. Now, some ministries within the movement do recommend a more broad-based program of study. But shouldn't a movement intending to encourage understanding of the Jewishness of the gospel, especially one this highly networked, draw on all the many resources available?

Practice

The Hebrew Roots movement presents itself partly as an educational movement. Indeed, some organizations, such as Brad Young's Gospel Research Foundation, seem to be more strictly educational in nature; it has sponsored conferences, one of which was held at Oral Roberts University, Our Lady of Sorrow Convent and Temple Israel in Tulsa, and included the participation of local rabbis and cantors.

Likewise, education is the focus of the mission statement of HaY'Did: "To train, educate and equip both the Jew and the non-Jew for study of the rich Biblical/Hebrew Heritage of our faith." But it is evident that HaY'Did is concerned with more than study. Their website continues: "HaY'Did (*The Friend* in Hebrew) is a neutral clearing house which reviews and stocks educational materials dealing in the subject matter of the Jewish roots of the Christian faith. In addition to providing our subscribers with these educational materials at the lowest possible price, HaY'Did sponsors various teaching seminars on the relationship of Biblical festivals and their relationship to Christian practice, and other teaching seminars all over the world."

Part of their educational thrust includes encouragement to certain practices. The Jewish holidays should be observed; the most "Biblically correct" period for worship is Friday night to Saturday night; Christmas, Easter and Halloween need to be "abandoned"—but HaY'Did is tolerant towards those who disagree.[5]

On the part of some Hebrew Roots organizations, there is a call to a "Torah-observant" or at least a "festival-observant" lifestyle as essential in the life of a Christian, as it brings the Christian into greater conformity with Jesus. As an example, reading the website of Awareness Ministry raises plenty of questions:"Feast day celebrations must not be limited to serving as mediums for worship and praise. We have discovered and aggressively teach that within these Biblical Memorial days such as Passover, Pentecost and Tabernacles is expressed every spiritual lesson that is needed to bring the Church to the knowledge of the full counsel of God."[6] Michael Rood of the program "A Rood Awakening" espouses a similar view. They are leaving out the fact that knowing Jesus is really the way to a relationship with God.

"Restoration"
Some in the Hebrew Roots movement encourage a "return" or a "restoration" of so-called "original" first-century Jewish practices. This necessitates a rejection of much else as non-Jewish and therefore wrong.This is wrongheaded both practically and theologically because:

• It is *not necessary* to observe Old Testament festivals as a means to a higher spirituality. The New Testament is clear that the Old Testament ceremonial laws, including the festivals, were pointers to the coming Messiah and were not intended for all time. Certainly the moral undergirdings of the Law of Moses are still in force, but the Hebrew Roots organizations seem more concerned with Sabbaths and festivals than with any other aspects of the Law.
• Neither is it *possible* in many cases to return to first-century practices. There is no longer a Temple or priesthood; the Church

is not the theocratic nation of Israel; and the culture has changed from that of a first-century agricultural world to a postmodern 21st-century world of technology and globalism.

• Nor is it *advisable* to try and observe Old Testament or first-century practices to the exclusion of other cultural forms. The Hebrew Roots movement shows little understanding that the gospel can function among various cultures. In essence, they function as a kind of Jewish variation on those Christian denominations that have sought to get back to "original New Testament Christianity." They confuse gospel content with culture. Thus, Garr's magazine says, ". . . practices which are not grounded in the Hebraic heritage of the faith of Jesus are not authentically Christian. They represent accretions which have been added from cultures which were founded on philosophies that are incompatible and inimical to the holistic worldview and mindset of the Biblical Hebrews."[7] But why can't "non-Hebraic" practices be acceptable, as long as they are not contrary to Scripture? The gospel can function across a multitude of cultures.

When it comes to excluding Christmas or Easter as pagan, we need to see that symbols can be sanctified. There were temples, priests and sacrifices before ancient Israel ever appeared on the scene, but God sanctified those pagan customs in the Old Testament. Even Christmas may have been originally instituted to *displace* the pagan holiday by offering a Christian alternative at the same time—not because Christianity became pagan.

One of the Hebrew Roots organizations, Awareness Ministry, says, "We declare the necessity of returning to the Old Testament for the purposes of establishing New Testament truth concerning moral and ethical standards as well as Biblical church orders. [We have seen] a dramatic increase of interest in such things as the use of banners in worship, dancing, the Christ centered celebration of Biblical feast days, observing the 'Hours of prayer', drawing lessons from Biblical Jewish customs and values that are impacting personal and family... many of these things are not essential to personal salvation, but they are *essential to growth* as we conform to the image of Christ, anticipating and preparing for Messiah's return [emphasis added]." [8]

Not only is Old Testament ceremonial worship not "essential to growth" under the New Covenant, but it is indeed questionable whether banners and dancing were typical of Old Testament worship. Sacrifices, priestly ministrations and singing were far more typical. The result of the above statement is that extra-biblical practices that have more in common with modern charismatic worship than Old Testament worship are called "essential to growth"—the very sort of thing the Hebrew Roots movement condemns.

In summary, while some organizations that place themselves within the Hebrew Roots movement may be sound biblically, many display some key problems. Beyond the most obvious one of advocating mandatory law-keeping (which usually seems to mean festival-keeping), there are other problems as displayed by some of the Hebrew Roots organizations:

• The movement's network includes both those who appear sound in Christology, soteriology and their view of Scripture, and those whose doctrine has been called into question in one or more of these areas, giving the impression that these are all evangelical Christian teaching ministries.
• The movement similarly shows little awareness that plenty of material has already been written on the Jewishness of the New Testament.

• Rather than being content with explicating the Jewish background as a way to understand the Biblical text, many wish to make first-century observances mandatory for the body of believers. The irony is that Christians simply cannot keep the law as it was kept in the first century, nor can they observe the festivals either as they were done in A.D. 30 or as they were done in 1000 B.C. The result is something quite removed from "original first-century" Jewish practices.

• The movement rejects anything that is allegedly "Greco-Roman," forgetting that the first-century church also grew up in such a context—with no call by the apostles for the Greco-Roman believers to "recover" their Jewish roots.

• The movement shows little understanding that the gospel can function among various cultures.

• The movement shows little interest in evangelism of Jewish people. Geographically, many of these organizations are removed from any substantial Jewish community.

Some in the Hebrew Roots movement are aware of problems with certain ministries and tendencies, and have spoken for a balanced view. Unfortunately, even among those who are not particularly engaged in controversial areas, some seem to lend tacit approval to those who are, by extensive networking via website links, conferences, and so on.

CONCLUSION

It is unwise to assume that all Hebrew Roots ministries are evangelical in doctrine. If you are interested in taking advantage of opportunities and resources to learn more about the Jewishness of the gospel from Jewish missions, Messianic congregations and good books, or from a Hebrew Roots organization, approach them with discernment. Jews for Jesus may be able to help evaluate particular resources.

Avoid any ministry where it seems that . . .
- people adulate (rather than appreciate) Jewishness or the teaching of rabbis
- people forsake Jesus for Jewishness
- Christians must observe Old Testament holidays and/or avoid celebrating Christmas and Easter, either because "God commanded it" or because it is seen as a superior path to lead one closer to God
- it is implied that by following certain worship practices one is returning to the worship of the early Church

Where many Hebrew Roots groups go astray is in their insistence that certain practices and preferences be made mandatory for all believers. As always, the Bible should be our first and foremost resource for determining which things are commanded and which are not.

FURTHER READING

Katz, Stephen., "The Jewish Roots Movement: Flowers and Thorns." *Havurah*, March/April, 2001. Published by Jews for Jesus http://www.jewsforjesus.org/publications/havurah/4_1/jewish roots

Daube, David., *The New Testament and Rabbinic Judaism*. Hendrickson, 1994. A classic by the late Jewish law professor at the University of California, Berkeley.

Mishkan: A Forum on the Gospel and the Jewish People 17-18, 1992-93. Issue devoted to "The Jerusalem School of Synoptic Studies." Articles pro and con, so you get both sides of the picture. Available by ordering online at: www.caspari.com/mishkan/contents/contents16.html#17-18.

Davies, W. D., *Paul and Rabbinic Judaism: Some Rabbinic Elements in Pauline Theology*. Philadelphia: Fortress

Press; or Sigler Press, 1980. A classic, though the average layperson will probably find it heavy reading.

ONLINE RESOURCES

http://www.isitso.org/guide/hebroot.html
A well-written response to the Hebrew Roots movement from a non-Jew and a former member of the Worldwide Church of God. It is quite extensive, and a good supplement to the material in this section. One of the most valuable sections is an exploration of the attraction that the Hebrew Roots movement holds for Christians from Sabbatarian and non-Sabbatarian backgrounds, followed by a word of personal testimony from the author, who is a Sabbatarian Christian in the Church of God.

http://www.empirenet.com/~messiah7/spl_rood.htm
A page about Michael Rood, prepared in 2003 by John Juedes, pastor of Messiah Lutheran Church of Palmdale, California.

Notes
1. http://graceandknowledge.faithweb.com/roots.html
2. The site in the previous footnote has as its banner sentence at the top of its web page, "A growing number of Christians are coming to an appreciation of the Jewish roots of Christianity and a love for the Sabbath and biblical festivals."
3. The site referred to above gives three reasons for this interest: the Holocaust, which has made Christians aware of anti-Semitism and the need to understand their Jewish neighbors; the increasing interest by Bible scholars in placing Jesus within the Jewish framework of His time; and the desire on the part of Christians to evangelize Jewish people. The Internet has helped this along, as most organizations in the movement now have a presence on the web and consequently the potential for a high profile and easy promulgation of their views.

4. Hanegraff, Hendrik H., "What's Wrong With The Faith Movement—Part One: E. W. Kenyon and the Twelve Apostles of Another Gospel." *Christian Research Journal* (Winter 1993), online at: http://www.iclnet.org/pub/resources/text/cri/cri-jrnl/web/crj0118a.html. See footnote 66.
5. See their "Statement of Tolerance," http://www.haydid.org/toleranc.htm
6. http://home.hiwaay.net/~aware/atglance.htm
7. http://www.restoremagazine.org/volume_1/122.htm
8. http://www.awarenessministry.org

Chapter Four
The "Two-House" Organizations

INTRODUCTION

One non-adherent describes the movement known as "Two-House" or "Messianic Israel," as centering on the idea that "the membership of the Church is largely made up of people who are descended physically from the lost tribes of Israel."[1] A more extended description is given by Angus and Batya Wootten, two of the more prominent proponents of the movement: "Messianic Israel deems the Jewish people to be the identifiable representatives and offspring of Judah and 'the children of Israel, his companions,' and that non-Jewish followers of the Messiah from all nations have been, up to now, the unidentifiable representatives and offspring of Ephraim and 'all the house of Israel, his companions.'"[2] In other words, non-Jewish believers are of one "house" of Israel, and Jewish believers are of the other "house"—hence, "Two-House" theology.

Put more bluntly, this movement maintains that Gentile Christians are beginning to realize their true identity as physical descendants of Israel.

The goal of the movement is stated as follows: "Messianic Israel is a people whose heart's desire is to fully reunite the olive tree of Israel—both branches— Ephraim and Judah—into one, redeemed, nation of Israel—through Messiah Yeshua. They seek to arouse Ephraim from obscurity, and by example, to awaken Judah to the Messiah—and thus to hasten both Yeshua's return to Earth and the restoration of the Kingdom to Israel."[3]

The Woottens' description indicates that "Messianic Israel" sees its role as helping to fulfill biblical prophecy of the "restoration" of the entire nation of Israel through non-Jewish believers recognizing their true descent, and thus being an example to the Jewish people.

A BIT OF BACKGROUND

Angus and Batya Wootten are generally recognized as the "founders" of "Messianic Israel."[4] Non-Jewish themselves, the Woottens became believers in Jesus in the 1970s and met up with many in the growing movement of Jews who were for Jesus. As they thought through the place of Jews and non-Jews in God's plan, they report that in their experience, Gentile Christians were treated like second-class citizens in the Messianic Jewish community. They write that Gentiles were "being rejected" by Messianic Judaism. They concluded that Scripture taught that there were two houses of Israel, Judah and Ephraim. In their books, they say that God is "restoring" the two houses, that Jewish believers are the house of Judah and non-Jewish or Gentile believers are the house of Ephraim.

Using Paul's statement in Romans 11:25, the Woottens' organization, Messianic Israel Ministries, writes that, "'blindness in part' has happened to all (both houses) of Israel, and as the blinders are lifted, non-Jewish followers in Yeshua will gain insight into their role as Ephraim, they will become defenders of Scriptural Torah and of Judah, and due to this character change, many Jewish people will accept Yeshua as Messiah. This process has already begun as indicated through the Messianic Jewish movement (Judah), the Christian Zionism movement (Ephraim), and the Messianic Israel movement (union of Judah and Ephraim)."[5] The Woottens publish a regular newsletter (*The House of David Herald*) and have authored several books vigorously advocating their viewpoint.

The 1980s saw the birth of Your Arms to Israel, headed by Moshe (or Marshall) Koniuchowsky based in Broward County, Florida. According to information at Koniuchowsky's website, his work began in New York City in 1984 as a Jewish evangelism agency called Messiah is God Ministries. An evangelism campaign was conducted in 1991 in South Florida under the name "Operation Joshua." Both he and his wife claim to be Jewish believers. Somewhere along the line they adopted the theology of "Messianic Israel," i.e., the "Two-House theory."

Koniuchowsky writes, "Messianic Nazarene Yisrael does in fact teach that Ephraim's seed has fulfilled the promise of physical multiplicity given to the patriarchs and views the re-gathering of the latter day 'gentiles,' as consisting mostly of lost Israelites."[6] And, "that Ephraim's recognition of their identity and restoration with brother Judah is the truth that will become the salvation of all Israel (Ezekial [sic] 37:16-28)."[7] It seems that this movement, which has a small but vocal following, teaches that rather than direct evangelism, the "coming out," so to speak, of Ephraim will lead to Israel's salvation.

IS IT HERESY?

Other names connected with the Two-House movement are David Hargis, Ed Chumney, and Monte Judah. One website contains a statement by Chumney and Judah regarding their theology and a response by Dan Juster, a Messianic Jewish author and pastor.[8] In their statement, Chumney and Judah speak of Two-House theology as part of the "Messianic/Hebrew roots movement." Juster disagrees with much that Chumney and Judah advocate, but concludes that, contrary to his earlier fear, they are not heretical.

Though the theological ideas expressed by the Woottens, Ed Chumney and the others may not be "heretical," they are

distinctly idiosyncratic and ultimately unbiblical. Take for
instance the umbrella organization, the Union of Nazarene
Yisraelite Congregations. In addition to advocating Two-House
theology, their website includes a statement of Torah-
observance and sacred-name theology. They have this to say:

> Today hundreds of thousands of unsaved and unbelieving
> traditional Jews and wayward Ephraimites continue to reside
> in all of Miami Beach from the North Miami Beach sight [sic]
> of our new facility down to South Beach, unable to relocate,
> with little or no Gospel witness representing the Messianic
> Nazarene Yisraelite movement. While there are still plenty of
> churches ready, willing and able to convert Jews, and
> reinforce Ephraim in pagan error, there are no known vibrant
> English speaking Messianic synagogues in Miami Beach. A
> true Messianic synagogue ordained by Yahweh must
> introduce Yahshua's blood atonement as the only means of
> eternal life, and the Torah as the only true basis and
> instruction manual for holy living by the redeemed
> community of Yahweh. Our restoration calling is
> commissioned to reintroduce the Father Yahweh's true
> eternal Name, as well as that of the Son of Yahweh.[9]

The "Two-House" movement can be criticized on several grounds:

1. Understanding of Bible Passages and Theology
Under the auspices of the International Messianic Jewish
Alliance, Kay Silberling, Daniel Juster and David Sedaca have
written a concise but thorough refutation of the teaching of
the Two-House movement.[10] In their paper they point out
several fallacies of interpretation. The Two-House movement
is wrong in asserting: (1) that the word *goy* always means
Gentile and that therefore Genesis 48:19 refers to Ephraim
becoming Gentiles; (2) that the number of descendants of
Abraham being as "the sand of the sea" precludes its

fulfillment by the Jewish people alone; (3) that the northern Israelites taken into captivity by Assyria are never called Jews.

In addition, the authors point out that the Woottens and Moshe Koniuchowsky present ambiguous evidence for all Christians in history being physical descendants of Israel. They also note that the basis for this claim is often entirely subjective on the part of the Gentile believer: Wootten says regarding how one can know if he or she is a physical descendant of Ephraim, "you knew in your 'knower.'"

Theologically, the "Two-House" proponents and organizations run the gamut from those that are theologically orthodox, except in their idiosyncratic doctrine of the Church, to those that are aberrant. Some that are evangelical regarding Christ hold to these views out of a misplaced desire to in some way have a greater connection with the Jewish people. Some have statements of faith that appear evangelical as to the person of Christ, though written in a kind of pseudo-Jewish nomenclature; other statements of faith are written in such a way that one cannot quite tell what they believe about the Trinity, the deity of Jesus and salvation.[11] At worst, some espouse non-evangelical theology and practices.

The Woottens believe in the deity of Jesus, and in salvation by faith in Him. One might almost overlook their idiosyncratic view of the relationship of Jews and non-Jews in the body of Christ, were they merely personal views. But now there is a whole "Two-House" network. Some organizations that are part of the movement promote Torah-observance or promulgate teachings on the alleged paganism of Christianity.

2. The Driving Question
The Two-House proponents are not alone in their desire to be part of the nation of Israel. Sadly, some non-Jews earnestly

wish that they were Jewish. For some of the motivations in this area, see: http://www.isitso.org/guide/hebroot.html, section "The Allure." [12]

The desire of the Woottens to see all believers in Jesus treated equally is an admirable one. But it would seem that the driving question from which the movement originated—how Gentiles can find acceptance among Jewish believers—has controlled their scriptural understanding, rather than scriptural understanding controlling their response to the perceived lack of acceptance.

3. Aberrant Ideas

The Your Arms to Israel site advertises a "Sefer Yahshar," [13] purporting to be the Book of Jasher mentioned occasionally in Scripture in such places as Joshua 10:13. Unfortunately, Koniuchowsky's claim that the book was first translated into English in 1840 is totally spurious. All existing claims to be the "Book of Jasher" are recent or spurious compositions. Yet Koniuchowsky offers this book and "is more convinced than ever, that this book or scroll in particular must and should be reinstated in the scriptures." Never mind that it never *was* in the Scriptures. He will include it in his Bible, known as the "Restoration Scriptures."

And what is the Restoration Scriptures? "We then proceeded to correct obvious anti-Yahshua redactions, shamefully tampered with by the Masoretic editors. Moreover, we reinserted the true Name back into this foundational source." [14]

Unlike many crafty translators and their translations that do not admit to an underlying agenda in their publications, *The Restoration Scriptures True Name Edition Study Bible* has an overriding and clear agenda in publishing this project. We admit that! ...We desire that *The Restoration Scriptures True Name Edition Study Bible* will lead to a repentance and return to YHWH for many, so as to experience life in His sight as a practicing Torah-keeping born-again Yisraelite.[15]

No reputable Bible scholar agrees that there is a legitimate Sefer Yahshar, nor that the biblical canon should be corrected, nor that the Masoretes were in grave error. This may not be theological heresy, but it does not speak well of the Hebrew Roots/Messianic Israel movement that it freely links to such resources as legitimate sources of knowledge and information.

4. Ingrown Nature
Just as problematic as the teaching about Ephraim and Judah is the fact that the movement has become ingrown, with its own conferences, directories,[16] music teams, speakers, etc., which mirror mainstream Messianic Jewish ministries. In essence, the movement has placed itself against, rather than alongside, other believers.

CONCLUSION
It's important to understand that the teaching that the visible Church is largely descended from the northern tribes cannot be substantiated historically or biblically. It's safe to say that Two-House movement adherents place far too much importance on trying to claim a Jewish identity. All believers in Jesus should be treated equally as full citizens within the body of Christ. Neither being Jewish nor descended from the tribes of Israel counts any more than being non-Jewish in God's sight.

FURTHER READING
Websites of Two-House Organizations:

House of David *aka* Messianic Israel Ministries (Angus and Batya Wootten)
http://www.mim.net/

Your Arms to Israel
http://yourarmstoisrael.org/

Responses:
Juster, Daniel C., "Is the Church Ephraim?" Previously available at http://www.umjc.org, but now only on the Wayback Machine:
http://web.archive.org/web/20000308231905/http://umjc.org/index.html
From there, click on "Documents" in the lower frame, then scroll for the link to the paper. *Counter-response:* We can also no longer locate online "Resolving Issues," by Angus Wootten.

"The Ephraimite Error:A Short Summary" by Kay Silberling, advised by Daniel Juster and David Sedaca. A concise and thorough refutation through an examination of the relevant biblical passages.
http://66.70.185.249/biblicaljudaism/EphraimiteErrorSummary.html

"The Ephramite Error," same authors, a longer version (PDF download)
http://66.70.185.249/biblicaljudaism/EphraimiteError.pdf
The most extensive response I have seen.

Counter-responses:
Koniuchowsky, Moshe Joseph, "The Truth About All Israel:A Refutation of the M.J.A.A. Position Paper on the Two Houses of Israel" (PDF):
http://yourarmstoisrael.org/The_Truth/THE_TRUTH_ABOUT_ALL_ISRAEL_by_Rabbi_Moshe_Koniuchowsky.pdf

The Messianic Israel Movement is mentioned with a brief critique in "Something Old, Something New:The Messianic Congregational Movement" by Bruce Lieske, Christian Research Journal 22:1 (June-August 1999). Available through the Christian Research Institute:
http://www.equip.org/free/DJ440.htm

Notes

1. Juster, Daniel C., "Is the Church Ephraim?" at:
http://web.archive.org/web/20000308231905/http://umjc.org/inde
x.html

2. http://www.mim.net/Beliefs.shtml

3. Ibid.

4. See http://www.mim.net/Who.shtml#Our%20History.

5. *We Declare These Truths to Be Self-Evident* (St. Cloud, FL:
Messianic Israel Alliance, 2002), at:
http://www.mim.net/Books/DeclaredTruths/WeDeclareScreen.pdf

6. http://yourarmstoisrael.org/Articles_new/restoration/
?page=12&type=10

7. http://yourarmstoisrael.org/misc/official_statements/
?page=doctrinal_statement&type=2

8. http://www.hebroots.org/twohousemeeting.htm

9. http://yourarmstoisrael.org/misc/?page=by/index

10. http://66.70.185.249/biblicaljudaism/EphraimiteErrorSummary.html

11. For example, see the Messianic Church of God in Royal Oak, MI, at:
http://www.messianics.us/statementoffaithMCOGfolder/StatementF
aith.htm, linked to from www.mim.net.

12. This site is compiled by someone affiliated with a Sabbatarian
Church of God denomination, but has much of value.

13. http://store.yourarmstoisrael.org/Qstore/
Qstore.cgi?CMD=011&PROD=1082997719

14. http://www.restorationscriptures.org/page.php?page=home

15. Ibid.

16. For example, http://www.mim.net/MIA/Directory/index.html

Chapter Five
The Hashivenu Group

INTRODUCTION

Within the structure of the Union of Messianic Jewish Congregations (see chapter 1.4), an organization called "Hashivenu," Hebrew for "bring us back" (to God), was formed in 1997. Its founders provide some of the theological direction for the movement. Hashivenu is a sort of think tank comprised of well-educated and theologically creative people, who have been calling for what they term a "mature Messianic Judaism." The theological and practical ideas emanating from Hashivenu have led to a good degree of ferment within the UMJC, so much so that some congregations have even pulled out.

What does Hashivenu mean by a "mature Messianic Judaism"? In their own words:

> We seek an authentic expression of Jewish life maintaining substantial continuity with Jewish tradition. However, Messianic Judaism is energized by the belief that Yeshua of Nazareth is the promised Messiah, the fullness of Torah. Mature Messianic Judaism is not simply Judaism plus Yeshua, but is instead an integrated following of Yeshua through traditional Jewish forms and the modern day practice of Judaism in and through Yeshua. Messianic Judaism will only attain maturity when it has established communal institutions which are capable of expressing its ideals and transmitting them effectively to ourselves, to our children, and to a skeptical world.[1]

In this chapter we'll unpack some of these ideas and see why Hashivenu is causing such ferment.

A BIT OF BACKGROUND

Hashivenu was formed by Stuart Dauermann, rabbi of Messianic congregation Ahavat Zion in Beverly Hills, California. The Hashivenu group includes Dauermann as President, G. Robert Chenoweth, Susan C. Chenoweth, Mark S. Kinzer, Richard C. Nichol, Ellen B. Quarry, Paul L. Saal and Michael H. Schiffman. Kinzer heads the Messianic Jewish Theological Institute (see Chapter 1.5 on educational institutions) and also leads congregation Zera Avraham in Ann Arbor, Michigan. Kinzer serves with the theology committee of the UMJC and has, for all practical purposes, become the leading theologian within Hashivenu. Nichol is rabbi of Congregation Ruach Israel in Needham, Massachusetts, while Saal heads Congregation Shuvah Yisrael in Simsbury, Connecticut. Both Nichol and Saal are part of the New England Messianic Jewish Council, whose address is that of Congregation Simchat Yisrael, headed by Tony Eaton, who also serves as treasurer for the UMJC. These congregational leaders are among the most articulate and erudite in the Messianic movement.

There is no one explicit platform or statement of theology that comes from Hashivenu, but there are some overarching ideas, chief of which has to do with identification with the Jewish community.

A QUESTION OF BELONGING

There have always been two somewhat competing positions in the Messianic movement concerning how Jewish believers in Jesus are to relate to the Jewish community at large. Some have been eager for the Jewish community to recognize the legitimacy of Jewish belief in Jesus and to grant validity to Jewish believers in Jesus. Much of the impetus for developing the Messianic congregational movement has been to "show" the Jewish community that we are "real" Jews; hence the trend to naming assemblies "synagogues," calling the leaders "rabbis," etc.

There is an important caveat here: not every expression of Jewishness on the part of Jewish believers or the Messianic community is intended to gain acceptance from the larger Jewish community. Jewish expression can be a personal statement or a matter of one's own convictions or community identification, regardless of how others respond. Some believe that maintaining a visible expression of Jewishness reflects the ongoing distinctiveness of the Jewish people in God's plan.

But when such expressions *are* intended to gain acceptance, how effective are they? At least one non-Messianic Jewish scholar, Dan Cohn-Sherbok, who has been a featured speaker at UMJC conferences, seems prepared to accept Messianic Judaism as a variety of Judaism in today's pluralistic world.[2] Yet it is unclear to what extent he would allow a theology that includes the Incarnation and the tri-unity of God to go under the rubric of Judaism. Another Jewish writer, Dennis Prager, has gone on record as affirming Messianic Jews as Jews, provided that they deny those doctrines.[3] Jewish author David Klinghoffer recently penned an article for the *Forward* reluctantly accepting the Jewishness of Jewish believers in Jesus on the grounds that it is inconsistent to accept secular Jews and not Messianic Jews.[4] Messianic Judaism is still far from being accepted in the mainstream Jewish world.

The other position taken by the Messianic movement has been described by detractors as "adversarial" and by others as being in the position of "underdog" or "outsider." These Messianic Jews do not hope for acceptance from the larger Jewish community, but in fact expect to *not* be accepted, just as Jesus and the apostles were largely rejected, and for that matter so were Moses and the prophets. In short, as Jesus was rejected (as prophesied in Isaiah 53), so His followers can expect the same. Some Jewish believers remember that when they came to faith, they attempted to continue attending their family synagogue in addition to Christian fellowships, in an attempt to maintain ties with their Jewish community. But once it was known that they were believers in Jesus, they were sometimes asked outright to leave.

These are broadly painted portraits of both views. And, as stated above, not every expression of Jewishness is a bid for acceptance. Some Jewish believers feel that they will always be a part of the Jewish community—accepted or not—and seek to live out a Jewish expression of their faith. As far as Hashivenu is concerned, they have strongly come down on the side of acceptance and seek to identify with the Jewish community in a way that goes beyond what most Jewish believers would considered necessary. For example, consider this statement on Messianic Jewish conversion by Tony Eaton, that both broaches the desire for acceptance and hints at the broader Hashivenu agenda of identifying almost entirely with the Jewish community:

> Can we ever expect acceptance from the wider Jewish community if we insist on bypassing the way that people have for centuries been received into the community? ... The challenge for our movement as we enter the new millennium is to develop and institute a conversion process for our non-Jewish members. Without this process, we will find it difficult—perhaps impossible—to *justify ourselves* as a Judaism to the wider Jewish community, the wider world, and perhaps in time, even to ourselves.[5] [emphasis added]

IMPLICATIONS FOR THEOLOGY AND PRACTICE

Kinzer, Dauermann, and Nichol all believe that the primary community to which a Jewish believer in Jesus must be committed is the Jewish people. By this they mean being a Jewish believer in Jesus means "locating" oneself, not primarily within the Church composed of both Jews and Gentiles, but within the Jewish community—even though a Jewish believer shares faith in Jesus with non-Jewish believers. Since the Jews are a people, "to be part of a people means embracing its history and tradition as one's own." [6] In Kinzer's words, Judaism is to be seen as "genus," and Messianic as "species."

It is from this basic premise that Hashivenu's core values are derived as follows:

1. Messianic Judaism is a Judaism, and not a cosmetically altered "Jewish-style" version of what is extant in the wider Christian community.
2. God's particular relationship with Israel is expressed in the Torah, God's unique covenant with the Jewish people.
3. Yeshua is the fullness of Torah.
4. The Jewish people are "us" not "them."
5. The richness of the Rabbinic tradition is a valuable part of our heritage as Jewish people.
6. Because all people are created in the image of God, how we treat them is a reflection of our respect and love for Him; therefore, true piety cannot exist apart from human decency.
7. Maturation requires a humble openness to new ideas within the context of firmly held convictions. [7]

A fuller explanation of these values is available on the Hashivenu website. It is not so much with these values that one might be inclined to take exception. However, other writings and statements from Hashivenu leaders have created cause for concern.

Implications for Ecclesiology (the Doctrine of the Church)

Mark Kinzer has been the one to set the theological agenda for Hashivenu and for the UMJC. In the past several years, Kinzer has developed a new ecclesiology that is quite different from traditional thinking.

Kinzer maintains that God made a covenant with the Jewish people, which is ongoing and continuous. Because that covenant still exists, all of its obligations and responsibilities exist as well. Therefore, God calls Jewish believers in Jesus to make the Jewish people their main community of commitment. And He calls all Jews to the obligations of observing the 613 commandments of the Torah.

According to Kinzer, Galatians 2:7-10 indicates that there was not only a separate mission for Jews and Gentiles, but also "two distinct sets of communities resulting from those missions, and two distinct leadership structures overseeing those missions and communities."[8] Kinzer calls this a "binitarian ecclesiology."[9] He concludes that the primary locus of a Jewish believer's community commitment is to the Jewish community; and that the primary locus of a Gentile believer's community commitment is to the Church. While both Jewish and Gentile believers in Jesus form aspects of the one people of God, they each have their own spheres of existence. They may come together in cooperation and make joint efforts, but there is *not* one unified Jewish-Gentile community of all believers. As Dauermann asserts on his web log, "Togetherness does not mean sameness."[10]

Rich Nichol underscores this emphasis when he writes that, "the irreducible dyad of human existence is Israel and the nations."[11] Commenting on this point, Dauermann states:

> The irreducible dyad that Rich Nichol mentions is intensely biblical. Why else, for example, would G-d have appointed and Scripture have highlighted two apostolates—one to the circumcision and the other to the uncircumcision (Galatians 2:9)? . . . in the purposes of God, it is only these two spheres which are mentioned, and they remain distinct.[12]

However, we would counter, the irreducible dyad of Scripture ultimately, and certainly clearly set forth in the New Testament, is the redeemed and the unredeemed.[13]

At least one person has concluded that the natural outworking of the Hashivenu point of view means there should be two separate religious systems, one for Jewish believers and one for non-Jews![14] While Kinzer and others have distanced themselves from any such statement, it's little wonder that this "binitarian" ecclesiology has led some in that direction and led others to reconsider the traditional (and we would argue biblical) doctrine of salvation.

Implications for Soteriology (the Doctrine of Salvation)

There are some in the Hashivenu ranks who have been less than forthcoming about the need of Jesus for salvation. While it may not have been stated explicitly, there is a concern that some within Hashivenu are prepared to allow for a *normative* salvation apart from conscious faith in Christ. Following are some questionable statements, the first from Mark Kinzer:

> Because of the validity of the Abrahamic covenant, I believe it's still as possible for a Jew who doesn't know Yeshua to have a living relationship with God, just as a Christian. But of course

Yeshua is still the Messiah and any Jew who knows him is in a better place and has more access to God than before.[15]

Kinzer also says:

We don't come as Christians bringing good news to damned souls who need to be delivered from religious bondage.[16]

Similarly, and somewhat patronizingly, Tony Eaton says:

Modern evangelicalism fixes on one aspect of things, it says if you say these four spiritual laws—that's your get out of jail free card. It says if you accept a certain concept of truth, this makes the difference for your eternal destiny. Not that I don't believe there's a certain amount of truth to that. Let me explain it this way. Among devout Jewish people, there's a concept called devakut, God consciousness, maybe Paul would say 'walking in the Spirit.' This is the highest achievement of a devout Jew. I don't think true devakut can be achieved without Messiah Yeshua, but you can get close, I suppose. But you can't get where you could have gotten.[17]

Kinzer clarified his quote above about the Abrahamic covenant in a letter addressed to Rich Robinson and Ruth Rosen who co-wrote an article for the *Havurah* publication on trends in the Messianic movement. In this letter he wrote:

Robinson and Rosen conclude that my statement "is clearly an example of two-covenant theology, which says that Jews already have a covenant with God through Abraham and so do not need Jesus in order to find salvation." Admittedly, such a statement could be an example of dual covenant theology, but it is not "clearly so." And, in the mouth of a Messianic Jewish leader, one can safely assume that there is probably a different way of construing the remark. Dual covenant theology holds that Jews and Christians have two distinct and equally valid paths to God: Christians come to God through the covenant established by Yeshua's sacrifice, whereas the relationship of Jews to God is through God's covenant with Abraham and his descendants. I do not know of any Messianic Jews who believe in dual covenant theology, for this theological framework has no place for Messianic Judaism. Despite raising the specter of "dual covenant theology," it appears that Robinson and Rosen also recognize that I do not embrace such a position, for they proceed to summarize my view as the belief that "God has already accepted them [i.e., non-Messianic Jews] *in Y'shua*" (emphasis mine).

I do believe that the Abrahamic covenant offers Jewish people access to God in and through Yeshua. That does not mean that all Jews, by virtue of being Jews, have a right relationship with God. It does mean that God's favor still rests upon Israel, and He makes a way for humble and faithful members of His people to enter His presence *through the unrecognized mediation of Israel's Messiah* (emphasis added).[18]

The phrase "unrecognized mediation" suggests that Kinzer holds to a form of inclusivism, according to which people may be saved through the work of Christ even if they have not professed conscious faith in Him. Inclusivism exists in various shades, and is associated (in one form or another) with the names of theologians such as John Hick, Karl Rahner and John Sanders.

On the other hand, the invocation of the Abrahamic covenant does have affinities to two-covenant theology, which was developed by mainstream Jewish philosopher Franz Rosenzweig in the early 20th century and adopted by some liberal theologians and even by some evangelical theologians.

According to two-covenant theology, the covenant with Abraham is a saving covenant. Non-Jews do need Jesus; Jews do not.

Kinzer's and Eaton's statements are ambiguous. Unlike some others, they add that it's better if one does believe in Jesus. Kinzer is a creative thinker and only time will tell the particulars of his views. As of this writing, he has a book forthcoming which will hopefully clarify his thinking and that of others (*Postmissionary Messianic Judaism: Redefining Christian Engagement with the Jewish People*, Brazos Press, November 2005).

There have been many responses written to two-covenant theology as well as to forms of inclusivism. We include some of the most helpful in the "Further Reading" sections of earlier chapters.

Implications for Evangelism

Stuart Dauermann's weblog criticizes certain aspects of evangelical Christianity as well as some in the Messianic Jewish movement, especially in regard to evangelism. He says that conservative evangelicals read Scripture through preconceived theological grids;[19] that the church sees the Great Commission, rather than the final consummation, as the be-all and end-all of God's will;[20] and that the church sees outreach more in terms of salesmanship than relationship.[21] While the accuracy of Dauermann's depiction is debatable, Mark Kinzer concurs and has been quoted as stating point blank that Jewish missions are obsolete.[22]

Dauermann and Kinzer are not the first to critique the Church or traditional methods of evangelism. Many churches have engaged in serious thought on the question of how relationships and proclamation interrelate, particularly those churches reaching postmodern seekers. This question is really part of the larger question framed by Richard Niebuhr, as to how Christ relates to culture.[23] To what extent should believers be involved in the world, seeking to transform it, living in it incarnationally? And to what extent are we *not* in the world, strangers and pilgrims, striving to live godly lives in the face of a sinful culture? Many would say the answer lies in a balance of both aspects; it is not a matter of either/or, but of both/and.

In Hashivenu's hierarchy, identification with the Jewish community comes before evangelism. There are both theological and sociological reasons for this. As opposed to some Jewish believers who discount most of the past 2,000 years of Jewish thought and history as having little value, Hashivenu wants to embrace this history as much as possible.[24] It then follows that traditional missions are wrong because they (supposedly) act like "outsiders" coming to proclaim a message. Kinzer and Dauermann would have Jewish believers in Jesus be such an integral part of the Jewish community that the message comes from "within." Whether such a proposal is realistic remains to be seen. After all, Jewish believers in Jesus were "insiders" in the first century, until the Jewish community effectively isolated them.[25] No Jewish believer in Jesus was seeking to be an "outsider," but we were labeled as such by the rest of the Jewish community.

Then there is a sociological reason for downplaying evangelism. Those who look for the Jewish community's acceptance sometimes eschew the more public forms of gospel proclamation and the discomfort they can bring, in favor of developing relationships with the Jewish community. Whether these relationships lead to proclamation is up for debate. However, for the Jewish believer who is not seeking inclusion in the Jewish community, forthright evangelism—public, one-on-one, as well as long-term relational interactions—is seen as an essential part of one's calling as a believer in Jesus.

Implications for Lifestyle and Relating to Jewish Tradition
According to Hashivenu's website:

> It is our conviction that HaShem brings Messianic Jews to a
> richer knowledge of himself through a modern day
> rediscovery of the paths of our ancestors—Avodah
> (liturgical worship), Torah (study of sacred texts), and
> Gemilut Chasadim (deeds of lovingkindness).[26]

Similarly, the fifth core value of Hashivenu is, "The richness of
the rabbinic tradition is a valuable part of our heritage as Jewish
people." In an elaboration on this statement, the writer states:

> Although weaned and wooed to believe that our New
> Covenant faith was based on the Bible and nothing but
> the Bible, "the only rule of faith and practice," we gradually
> discovered that living out our faith inevitably had a
> cultural component. The Bible cannot be understood
> apart from a community context, which helps one
> understand its deepest meanings. In this way, obedience
> might become incarnate in daily life. We realized that
> having our views shaped entirely by a non-Jewish context
> was leaving a foreign imprint on our hearts, minds and
> lives. . . . We also began to appreciate how our own
> spiritual lives stood to benefit from the fruit of thousands
> of years of Jewish struggle for understanding.

Those committed to the Hashivenu vision place high
importance on rabbinic thought. The problem, though, is
that rabbinic thought and writing are double-edged. Much
rings right and true, especially in the areas of ethics, liturgy
and some biblical commentary. However, much is also a
departure from biblical teaching. Rabbinic Judaism came
into being after A.D. 70 as a top-to-bottom reworking   of
Judaism without a Temple and a priesthood. As rabbinic

Judaism continued to develop, it was influenced by factors such as its need to stand in opposition to Jewish believers in Jesus and to the gospel message. It was further influenced by Greek philosophy in medieval times, and whole areas of modern Judaism, such as the Kabbalah, are closer to Gnosticism than to biblical faith. (Kabbalah is the system of Jewish mysticism.)

It is a matter of practical theology how a Jewish believer in Jesus should relate to this accumulation of traditions, commentaries, liturgies, ways of thinking and cultural forms in Judaism. (Note here that we are not talking about relating to biblical material, such as the Law of Moses, but to the traditions of the past 2,000 years.) The fact is that many Jewish believers in Jesus find much of value in Jewish tradition, culture, and ceremonies. Many embrace what they can and perhaps find some significance that has to do with their faith in Jesus. But Hashivenu advocates much more than that. They have made it a matter of foundational theology. Hashivenu's postulation of a "binitarian" theology of the Church does not leave it an open matter; in their view, Jewish believers *must* identify first and foremost with the Jewish community, and therefore *must* accord legitimacy to the past 2,000 years of the development of Judaism. "Legitimacy," however, is a slippery word. It remains to be seen whether Hashivenu wants to accord the entire history of Jewish tradition and teaching the status of "truth," or whether they only intend to find value in it as they can. For instance, it is unclear whether Hashivenu will move to the point of accepting the authority of rabbinic tradition for determining how we are to live our lives today.

CONCLUSION

In a way, the position being delineated by the Hashivenu group is comfortable. If there are two separate tracks for Jewish and Gentile believers in Jesus, then many of the

tough practical questions that have come up in the
Messianic movement are no longer problematic. If
evangelism is thought of as not urgent, and accepting Jesus
something that just gives an "extra" to one's existing
relationship with God, then conflict with the larger Jewish
community effectively disappears.

The leaders of Hashivenu are intelligent and they articulate their
views well. They model a level of thinking to which most
Messianic congregations would do well to aspire. Many in the
Messianic movement would also do well to heed Hashivenu's call
for leaders to be well educated, and for the title "rabbi" to stop
being used by those who are untrained. And many Jewish
believers might do well to think about the best ways for them to
identify with their Jewish people. And so far the Hashivenu group
has affirmed the cardinal doctrines of God's tri-unity and the deity
of Y'shua. (See chapter 2.1 for the Jewishness of these doctrines.)

But in relation to ecclesiology, evangelism and theology, it is
reasonable to be concerned that Hashivenu is distancing itself
from the rest of the body of Messiah (though in their view
they are doing exactly what God wants for Jewish believers).
This runs contrary to the unity between Jew and Gentile that
is available to us in Jesus and to which we are called.

Furthermore, Kinzer speaks of Messianic Judaism as one
form of Judaism, other forms of which are also "valid" (a
word that can mean many things). Whatever "valid" or
"legitimate" might mean, it seems to include the perspective
that modern Judaism is as "OK" as the gospel. Kinzer has yet
to spell out the full implications of this for his thinking, but
his book (forthcoming at this time of writing) may unpack
things further.[27] The biggest cause for concern here is that
in Hashivenu's quest for acceptance within the Jewish
community, they "will be tempted to give back recognition
and approval."[28]

FURTHER READING

Kinzer, Mark S., *The Nature of Messianic Judaism: Judaism as Genus, Messianic as Species*. West Harford, CT: Hashivenu Archives, no date. Summarizes Mark Kinzer and Hashivenu's viewpoint.

Kinzer, Mark S., *Postmissionary Messianic Judaism: Redefining Christian Engagement with the Jewish People*. Brazos Press. Forthcoming, November 2005.

Robinson, Rich and Ruth Rosen, "The Challenge of Our Messianic Movement, Part One," *Havurah* 6:2 (May 2003), at http://www.jewsforjesus.org/publications/havurah/6_2/challenge1

Robinson, Rich and Ruth Rosen, "The Challenge Of Our Messianic Movement, Part 2" *Havurah* 6:3 (August 2003), at http://www.jewsforjesus.org/publications/havurah/6_3/challenge2

Nash, Ronald, *Is Jesus the Only Savior?* Grand Rapids: Zondervan, 1994.

Richard, Ramesh, *The Population of Heaven: A Biblical Response to the Inclusivist Position on Who Will Be Saved*. Chicago: Moody Press, 1994.

Notes

1. http://www.hashivenu.org
2. Cohn-Sherbok, Dan, *Messianic Judaism*. Cassell, 2000.
3. Prager, Dennis, "A new approach to Jews for Jesus." *Moment*, Jun 30, 2000 (Vol 25, No 3), pp. 28-29.
4. Klinghoffer, David, "The Disputation: Are We Being Fair to Messianic Jews?" http://www.forward.com/articles/3280, dated June 10, 2005.

5. Eaton, Tony, "A Case for Jewish Leadership," in *Voices of Messianic Judaism*, Dan Cohn-Sherbok, Ed. Baltimore: Lederer/Messianic Jewish Publishers, 2001, p. 121.

6. Kinzer, Mark. S., *The Nature of Messianic Judaism: Judaism as Genus, Messianic as Species* (West Harford, CT: Hashivenu Archives, no date), p. 17.

7. http://www.hashivenu.org/core_values.htm

8. Kinzer, p. 38.

9. Ibid., p. 39.

10. "The Real Identity of the One New Man" at: http://rabbenu.blogspot.com

11. Rich Nichol, as quoted in "Defining Messianic Judaism," UMJC Theology Committee, Summer 2002, Commentary by Russ Resnik available at:
http://www.umjc.org/main/faq/definition/ResnikCommentary.pdf

12. http://www.jewsforjesus.org/publications/havurah/7_1/letters

13. Ibid.

14. Blog of Sean Emslie, who attends Stuart Dauermann's congregation:
http://towardblog.blogspot.com/2005_02_01_towardblog_archive.html, posting for February 9, 2005, entitled, "2 Religions—1 Messiah." His extensive blog has a number of posts distancing "Messianic Judaism" from "Jews for Jesus" and "mission" groups.

15. As cited by Gabriela Karabelnik in "Competing Trends in Messianic Judaism: The Debate over Evangelicalism," unpublished senior thesis, Department of Religious Studies, Yale University, 2002, note 203, "Kinzer interview."

16. Ibid., note 212.

17. Ibid., note 204, "Eaton interview."

18. *Havurah* 7:1 (February, 2004) available at:
http://www.jewsforjesus.org/publications/havurah/7_1/letters

19. http://rabbenu.blogspot.com, post "Toward an Expansive Biblicism," January 23, 2005.

20. Ibid. "This is a revolutionary truth . . . however, the Church has generally been blind to this."

21. Ibid., "Toward a New Paradigm of Messianic Jewish Outreach," January 2, 2005.

22. Pardo-Kaplan, Deborah, "Jacob vs. Jacob: Jewish Believers in Jesus Quarrel over Both Style and Substance," in *Christianity Today*, February 2005. Accessed online at: http://www.christianitytoday.com/ct/2005/002/31.76.html. Does Kinzer mean missions to Jews only? He is quoted as saying: "I think they should be dismantled," Kinzer says. "I think that whatever constructive role they may have played in the past, times have changed. For the present situation and the future, I see missions as primarily an obstacle."

23. Niebuhr, H. Richard, *Christ and Culture*. HarperSanFrancisco, 1956.

24. It is not clear what Hashivenu will have to say about the rabbinic oral law, without which there is little guidance in Judaism in how to observe the 613 commandments in modern times.

25. Primarily in the "birkat ha-minim," the "blessing on the heretics," which was recited in the late first-century synagogue to exclude various groups, including Jews who believed in Jesus. Also following the Bar Kochba war of A.D. 132-135—which was fought under the platform that Rabbi Akiva was the Messiah—something Jewish believers in Jesus could not accept.

26. http://www.hashivenu.org. "HaShem" is an Orthodox Jewish way of referring to God, literally, "the Name."

27. Kinzer, Mark S., *Postmissionary Messianic Judaism: Redefining Christian Engagement with the Jewish People*, Brazos Press. Announced date, November 2005.

28. Klett, Fred, "The Centrality of Messiah and the Theological Direction of the Messianic Movement," Proc. of LCJE-NA Conference, 2002, Orlando. (http://www.lcje.net/papers/2002.html). Also Gabriela Karabelnik, "Competing Trends": "One of the central challenges of the UMJC involves balancing how much to strive for recognition and acceptance from the Jewish community versus how much to give back—if too much is given; its own existence becomes relativized," section "Conclusion: Some Challenges Ahead."

Appendices

Appendix A
A Word or Two about Nazarene Judaism

Mention should also be made of "Nazarene Judaism," a movement that in the United States is most closely identified with a man named James Scott Trimm. This is not to be confused with the Protestant denomination known as the Church of the Nazarene.

Nazarene Judaism believes Jesus to be the Messiah—but the available statements of faith are not in any way recognizably evangelical when it comes to the person of Christ or the Trinity. Trimm's website explains the nature of God in this way: "We believe that YHWH reveals Himself in many ways, characteristics and sefirot, including those of Father, Word (Memra), and the Ruach HaKodesh (Holy Spirit)."[1]

The statement that God "reveals" Himself in many ways is entirely different than the evangelical doctrine that God exists in three persons. The term "sefirot" is in fact borrowed from Kabbalah (Jewish mysticism), which teaches that God exists in ten emanations called *sefirot*. Another Nazarene Judaism website specifically identifies the Trinity as a pagan doctrine.[2]

In other areas of doctrine, Nazarene Judaism:

- believes in the necessity to observe the Torah. It is a kind of "restorationist" movement: "Today we are seeking to put Y'shua back into the context of first century Judaism. Nazarene Judaism is a spiritual renaissance, a revival, a return to the pure faith of first century Nazarenes."[3]
- believes in an original non-Greek New Testament. As a corollary, Trimm does not believe in the doctrine of inerrancy: "In addition to grammatical errors in the Greek New Testament, there are also a number of 'blunders' in the text

which prove that the present Greek text is not inerrant." [4]
• does not believe the New Covenant is for today: "The
truth is that the New Covenant is not the Good News
(Gospel) but is a covenant which HaShem will make with
the House of Israel and the House of Judah' when He
establishes the Kingdom. There is nothing in the Scriptures
to indicate that there is more than one New Covenant." [5]

Further insight into Nazarene Judaism's theological
orientation can be gained from looking at their teaching
institute, which they call a yeshiva. Under a listing of
theology courses offered, we find:

> Advanced Systematic Theology—Jewish Mysticism I-
> This course will cover Jewish mysticism, especially in
> relationship to understanding the Godhead. Textbook:
> MYSTERY OF THE GODHEAD; BASIC CONCEPTS OF
> KABBALAH available from SANJ. [6]

The Kabbalah, however, is radically unbiblical, teaching concepts
such as reincarnation, the existence of God in ten emanations or
sefirot, and an explanation of evil and redemption remarkably at
variance with the Bible's story. [7] Another Nazarene Judaism
website (in which the movement is called Netzarim Judaism—
Netzarim being Hebrew for Nazarene) garnishes its front page
with a chart of the ten kabbalistic sefirot and a list of Kabbalistic
books on the side. Nothing could be further from biblical
teaching and certainly should not be called "Messianic Jewish."

Yet, adherents to Nazarene Judaism identify as Jewish and
appear to be content to be called "Messianic Jews":

> *SHOULD NAZARENES DENY BEING "MESSIANIC JEWS"?*
> Absolutely not! Although the term is scripturally inaccurate, we
> are Jews who believe in Messiah. In fact any Jew who believes

in the concept of "Messiah" (even if that "Messiah" is not Yeshua) might reasonably be termed a "Messianic Jew." So we need not deny that we are "Messianic Jews" to those who ask.[8]

It is not clear whether Trimm was born Jewish; according to his website, he "began practicing normative Rabbinic Judaism at the age of fourteen. At the age of eighteen, James concluded that Yeshua of Nazareth had been the Messiah of Judaism."[9] He does not spell out in detail what he came to believe about Jesus. He claims to have received a doctoral degree from Saint John Chrysostom Theological Seminary, which claims to be affiliated with the Catholic Apostolic Church of North America. (For more on Trimm's qualifications, see the Further Reading section.)

Besides teaching Kabbalah, it is instructive that a course called "Answering Christendom" is taught alongside courses in "Answering Islam" and "Answering Mormonism."

Nazarene groups are sometimes listed under a "Messianic" heading in online search engines. Theologically, though, Nazarene Judaism is well outside the pale of the Messianic movement.

FURTHER READING
On James Trimm:
> Doctor James Scott Trimm
> http://www.seekgod.ca/trimmdoc.htm
>
> Saint John Chrysostom Theological Seminary
> http://www.seekgod.ca/saintjohn.htm
>
> James Trimm as Rabbi Yosef
> http://www.seekgod.ca/rabbiyosef.htm

On the Kabbalah:
> "Kabbalah: Fact or Fiction," *ISSUES* 12:2
> http://www.jewsforjesus.org/publications/issues/12_2/kabbalah

"A History of the Kabbalah," *ISSUES* 12:2
http://www.jewsforjesus.org/publications/issues/12_2/
kabbalahhistory

Notes

1. http://www.nazarene.net/Statement.htm
2. http://www.nazarite.net/answer-18.html
3. Trimm, James Scott, "What is Nazarene Judaism?" Online at:
http://www.unjs.org/what_is_nazarene_judaism.htm
4. Trimm, *Nazarene Jewish Manifesto*, p. 58, available as a PDF
download at: http://www.unjs.org/NazareneJudaismManifesto.pdf
5. http://www.nazarene.net/newcovenant.htm
6. http://www.nazarene.net/yeshiva/course_descriptions.htm
(emphasis in the original)
7. In one popular form of the Kabbalah, original "shells" broke,
emptying divine "sparks" to earth. To achieve redemption, man must
work according to Torah and "raise the sparks" back to heaven.
8. Trimm, *Manifesto*, p. 7.
9. http://www.trimmfamily.com/JamesSTrimm.html

Appendix B
More Recommended Reading

For your convenience, we have listed all the URLs cited in this book at: http://www.jewsforjesus.org/publications/fieldguide

History and Theology: Jewish Believers in Jesus and Missions

Ariel, Yaacov, *Evangelizing the Chosen People: Missions to the Jews in America, 1880-2000*, Chapel Hill, NC: University of North Carolina Press, 2000. A comprehensive and unusually sympathetic survey of the history of modern Jewish evangelism in the U.S. written by a non-Jesus-believing Jew.

Cohn-Sherbok, Dan, *Messianic Judaism*. New York: Cassell, 2000. A non-Jesus-believing rabbi describes the history and beliefs of the modern Messianic movement, arguing for the authenticity of Messianic Judaism as a legitimate branch of Judaism within a pluralist model.

Fruchtenbaum, Arnold, *Hebrew Christianity: Its Theology, History and Philosophy*. Tustin, CA: Ariel Ministries Press, 1983. Gives a theological basis for Hebrew Christianity and practical suggestions for Hebrew-Christian (now more commonly called Messianic Jewish) identity and practice.

Gundry, Stanley N. & Louis Goldberg, eds. *How Jewish is Christianity: Two Views on the Messianic Movement*. Grand Rapids: Zondervan, 2003. A discussion of the rationale, biblical basis and practice of Messianic faith and Messianic Judaism.

Harris-Shapiro, Carol, *Messianic Judaism: A Rabbi's Journey Through Religious Change in America*. Beacon Press, 1999. A Reconstructionist rabbi offers insight, history and observation.

Maoz, Baruch, *Judaism is Not Jewish: A Friendly Critique of the Messianic Movement*. UK: Mentor: Christian Focus Publications and Christian Witness to Israel, 2003. A critical survey of the theology and practice of the Messianic movement in Israel and the U.S.

Pritz, Ray, *Nazarene Jewish Christianity: From the End of the New Testament Period Until Its Disappearance in the Fourth Century*, Leiden: E.J. Brill, 1988. A historical study of Jewish Christians in the early centuries.

Sevener, Harold A., *A Rabbi's Vision: A Century of Proclaiming Messiah, A History of Chosen People Ministries*, Charlotte, NC: Chosen People Ministries, 1994. A history of one of the older U.S. Jewish missions.

Stern, David H., *Messianic Jewish Manifesto*. Jerusalem: Jewish New Testament Publications, 1988. One approach to the theological development of Messianic Judaism.

Tucker, Ruth A., *Not Ashamed: The Story of Jews for Jesus*. Sisters, OR: Multnomah Publishers, 1999. A missiologist and historian provides background and analysis of the people and methods used in the first 25 years of this Jewish mission.

"Jewish Evangelism: A Call to the Church," Lausanne Occasional Paper No. 60, produced by the Issue Group on this topic at the 2004 Forum for World Evangelization, hosted by the Lausanne Committee for World Evangelization in Pattaya, Thailand, September 29 to October 5, 2004
Available at:
http://community.gospelcom.net/lcwe/assets/LOP60_IG31.pdf

Resources for Jewish Ministry
Brown, Michael L., *Answering Jewish Objections to Jesus*. Grand Rapids: Baker Books, 2000, 2003. In three volumes. The

most comprehensive books of Jewish apologetics since the early twentieth century. A fourth volume is planned.

Cohen, Steve, *Beginning from Jerusalem*, St. Louis: Apple of His Eye Mission Society, 2001. A Jewish believer in Jesus and mission leader offers insights about Jewish evangelism, especially for American Lutherans.

Goldberg, Louis, *Our Jewish Friends*. Neptune, NJ: Loizeaux Brothers, 1977. Advice on Jewish evangelism from a scholarly Jewish believer in Jesus, who once headed the Jewish Studies program at Moody Bible Institute, Chicago.

Rosen, Moishe and Ceil, *Witnessing to Jews*, San Francisco: Purple Pomegranate Productions, 1998. A practical handbook of creative lessons on Jewish evangelism written for Christians by a modern missionary pioneer and his wife.

Wan, Enoch and Tuvya Zaretsky, *Jewish-Gentile Couples: Trends, Challenges and Hopes*, Pasadena: William Carey Library, 2004. Research into the difficulties encountered by Jewish-Gentile couples with insight and some practical strategies for ministry to them.

Periodicals

Mishkan: A Forum on the Gospel and the Jewish People, Jerusalem: Caspari Center for Biblical and Jewish Studies. A journal dedicated to biblical and theological thinking on issues related to Jewish evangelism, Hebrew-Christian/Messianic-Jewish identity, and Jewish-Christian relations.

Kesher, Albuquerque, NM: Union of Messianic Jewish Congregations. A journal of Messianic Judaism which provides a forum to address the issues that face contemporary Messianic Judaism.

The Messianic Times. International Messianic newspaper published six times a year.

Messianic Jewish Life (archives only).

Boundaries (archives only).

ISSUES: A Messianic Jewish Perspective. A bimonthly mini-magazine for Jewish believers and seekers.

Havurah (formerly *Mishpochah Message*). A quarterly publication for the Jewish believing community.

Messianic Good News. Prophecy and other Scripture articles are contained in this newsletter.

Israel, My Glory. Articles on Israel and prophecy, published bimonthly.

Appendix C
LCJE Member Organizations

Celebrate Messiah, Australia

Jews for Jesus, Canada

Den Danske Israelsmission, Denmark

Israelsmissionens Unge, Denmark

The Faroese Israel Mission, Faroe Islands

Finnish Evangelical Lutheran Mission, Finland

Finnish Lutheran Mission, Finland

Patmos, Finland

Evangeliumsdienst für Israel, Germany

Beit Sar Shalom, Germany

Caspari Center, Israel

LCJE Japan

Den Evangeliske Lutherske Frikirkes Israelsmisjon, Norway

Norwegian Church Ministry to Israel, Norway

AMZI, Switzerland

Board for Israel of the NRC, The Netherlands

Church's Ministry among Jewish People (CMJ), United Kingdom

Christian Witness to Israel (CWI), United Kingdom

Ariel Ministries, USA

CJF Ministries, USA

International Messianic Jewish Alliance, USA

Hope of David, USA

Messiah Now Ministries, USA

Jews for Jesus, USA

Tikkun Ministries, Inc., USA

Not included is a list of individual members who represent
other organizations, as such a list would be too long.

Appendix D
Judaism 101

THE THREE MAIN BRANCHES OF JUDAISM

The three divisions mentioned in this chart are not denominations. They are more like associations, with classifications according to cultural and doctrinal formulas. Within each branch you will find adherents with varying degrees of observance. Many Jewish people formulate their own informal version of Judaism, and do not fit strictly into any one of these categories. Nevertheless, the information in the chart below should be helpful.

CATEGORY	Orthodox	Conservative	Reform
History	Orthodoxy dates back to the days of the Talmud (2nd to 5th centuries A.D.). Orthodoxy today seeks to preserve classical or traditional Judaism.	Conservative Judaism emerged in the 19th Century Germany as a reaction to the assimilationist tendencies of Reform Judaism. It tried to be a middle ground, attempting to maintain basic traditions while adapting to modern life.	Reform Judaism emerged following the emancipation from ghetto life in the late 18th century. It sought to modernize Judaism and thus stem the tide of assimilation threatening German Jewry.
Other Terms	Traditional or Torah Judaism	Historical Judaism	Liberal or Progressive Judaism

CATEGORY	Orthodox	Conservative	Reform
View of Scripture	Torah is truth, and we must have faith in its essential, revealed character. A true Jew believes in revelation and the divine origin of the oral and written Torah.	The Bible is the word of God and man. It is not inspired in the traditional sense, but rather dynamically inspired. Revelation is an ongoing process in the evolutionary sense.	Revelation is a continuous process. Torah is a human document preserving the history, culture, legends and hope of a people. It is valuable for deriving moral and ethical insights
View of God	God is spirit rather than form. He is a personal God: omnipotent, omniscient, omnipresent, eternal and compassionate.	The concept of God is non-dogmatic and flexible. There is less atheism in Conservative Judaism than in Reform, but most often God is considered impersonal and ineffable.	Reform Judaism allows a varied interpretation of the "God concept" with wide latitude for naturalists, mystics, supernaturalists or religious humanists. It holds that "the truth is that we do not know the truth."
View of Man	People are morally neutral, with good and	This group tends toward the Reform view,	Human nature is basically good. Through

CATEGORY	Orthodox	Conservative	Reform
View of Man (cont.)	evil inclinations. They can overcome their evil bents and be perfected by their own efforts in observation of the Law.	though it is not as likely to espouse humanism. Perfectibility can come through enlightenment. Humanity is "in partnership" with God.	education, encouragement and evolution humans can actualize the potential already existing within them. Humankind may be God.
View of Sin	Orthodox Jews do not believe in "original sin." Rather, one commits sin by breaking the commandments of the Law.	Conservative Jews do not believe in "original sin." The individual can sin in moral or social actions.	Reform Jews do not believe in "original sin." Sin is reinterpreted as the ills of society.
View of Salvation	Repentance (belief in God's mercy), prayer and obedience to the Law are necessary for salvation.	Conservative Jews tend toward the Reform view, but include the necessity of maintaining Jewish identity.	Salvation is obtained through the betterment of self and society.
View of the Tradition of the Law	The Law is the essence of Judaism. It is authoritative and	Adaptation to contemporary situations is inevitable. The	The law is an evolving ever-dynamic religious code that adapts

CATEGORY	Orthodox	Conservative	Reform
View of the Tradition of the Law (cont.)	gives structure and meaning to life. The life of total dedication to Halakhah (Jewish Law) leads to a nearness to God.	demands of morality are absolute. The specific laws are relative.	to every age. They maintain, "If religious observances clash with the just demands of civilized society, then they must be dropped."
View of Messiah	The Messiah is a personal, super-human being who is not divine. He will restore the Jewish kingdom and extend his righteous rule over the earth. He will execute judgment and right all wrongs.	Conservative Jews hold much the same view as the Reform.	Instead of belief in Messiah as a person or divine being, they favor the concept of a Utopian age toward which mankind is progressing.
View of Life After Death	There will be a physical resurrection. The righteous will exist forever with God in the Garden of Eden. The unrighteous will suffer, but	Conservative Jews tend toward the Reform view, but are less influenced by Eastern thought.	Generally, Reform Judaism has no concept of personal life after death. They say a person lives on in the accomplishments or in the minds of

CATEGORY	Orthodox	Conservative	Reform
View of Life After Death (cont.)	disagreement exists over their ultimate destiny.		others. There is some similarity to Eastern thought, where souls merge into one great impersonal life force.
Distinctives in Synagogue Worship	The synagogue is a house of prayer; study and social aspects are incidental. All prayers are recited in Hebrew. Men and women sit separately. The officiants face the same direction as the congregants.	The synagogue is viewed as the basic institution of Jewish life. Alterations listed under Reform are found to a lesser degree in Conservative worship.	The Synagogue is known as a "Temple." The service has been modernized and abbreviated. English, as well as Hebrew, is used. Men and women sit together. Reform temples use choirs and organs in their worship services.

RECONSTRUCTIONIST JUDAISM

Reconstructionists believe that Judaism is an "evolving religious civilization." In one way, it is *more* liberal than Reform Judaism: the movement does not believe in a personified deity that is active in history and does not believe that God chose the Jewish people. In another way, Reconstructionist Judaism is *less* liberal than Reform Judaism: Reconstructionists observe *halakhah* (Jewish Law) if they *choose* to, not because it is a binding Law from God, but because it is a valuable cultural remnant.

CHASIDISM

This "Ultra-Orthodox" Jewish sect, founded in 18th century Europe by the Ba'al Shem Tov, believes that acts of kindness and prayer can be used to reach God, as opposed to the older view that one could only become a righteous Jew through rigorous learning. The word Chasid describes a person who does *chesed* (good deeds for others). Chasidic Jews dress distinctively, live separately from modern society, and are dedicated to strict observance of Jewish Law. They have also preserved the "mystical" foundations of Jewish theology, such as kabbalah.

SOME COMMON TERMS IN JUDAISM THAT WILL BE HELPFUL TO KNOW AS YOU EXPLORE THE MESSIANIC MOVEMENT:

Ashkenazic Jews (ahsh-ken-AH-zik) or Ashkenazim (ahsh-ken-ah-ZEEM)
Jews from eastern France, Germany and Eastern Europe, and their descendants. Most Jews in America are Ashkenazic.

Kabbalah (kuh-BAH-luh)
Literally, tradition. Jewish mystical tradition.

Mikvah (MIK-vuh)
Lit. gathering. A ritual bath used for spiritual purification. It is used primarily in conversion rituals and after the period of sexual separation during a woman's menstrual cycles, but many Chasidim immerse themselves in the mikvah regularly for general spiritual purification. The Messianic movement sometimes incorporates this tradition in public profession of faith through immersion.

Oral Torah (TOH-ruh) or Mishnah
Jewish teachings explaining and elaborating on the Written Torah, handed down orally until the 2nd century A.D., when they began to be written down in what became the Talmud.

Rabbi (RAB-bye)
A religious teacher and person authorized to make decisions on issues of Jewish law. Also performs many of the same functions as a Protestant minister.

Ruach HaKodesh The Holy Spirit

Sephardic Jews (s'-FAHR-dic) or Sephardim (seh-fahr-DEEM)
Jews from Spain, Portugal, North Africa and the Middle East and their descendants.

Shofar (sho-FAHR)
A ram's horn, blown like a trumpet as a call to repentance.

Shul (SHOOL)
The Yiddish term for a Jewish house of worship. The term is used primarily by Orthodox Jews.

Siddur (SID-r; sid-AWR) Lit. order. Prayer book.

Synagogue (SIN-uh-gahg)
From a Greek root meaning "assembly." The most widely accepted term for a Jewish house of worship. The Jewish equivalent of a church, mosque or temple.

Tallit (TAH-lit; TAH-lis)
A shawl-like garment worn during morning services, with *tzitzit* (long fringes) attached to the corners as a reminder of the commandments. Sometimes called a prayer shawl.

Talmud (TAHL-mud)
The most significant collection of the Jewish oral tradition interpreting the Torah

Tanakh (tuhn-AHKH)
Acronym of Torah (Law), Nevi'im (Prophets) and Ketuvim

(Writings). Written Torah; what non-Jews call the Old Testament.

Temple
1) The central place of worship in ancient Jerusalem, where sacrifices were offered, destroyed in A.D. 70

2) The term commonly used for houses of worship within the Reform movement.

Torah (TOH-ruh)
In its narrowest sense, Torah is the first five books of the Bible: Genesis, Exodus, Leviticus, Numbers and Deuteronomy (sometimes called the Pentateuch). In its broadest sense, Torah is the entire body of Jewish teachings.

Yarmulke (YAH-mi-kuh)
From Tartar "skullcap," or from Aramaic "Yirei Malka" (fear of the King). The skullcap head covering worn by Jews during services, and by some Jews at all times.

Y'shua (sometimes spelled Yeshua) Jesus

Zionism (ZYE-uhn-ism)
A political movement to create and maintain a Jewish state. The word is derived from Zion, another name for Jerusalem.

Appendix E
A Rationale for Jewish Evangelism

What happens when the most loving thing you can do is tell someone something they do not want to hear? How do you tell someone something that is crucial to their welfare, when they think they know what you are going to say and they have already decided it does not apply to them? Is there ever a right time to say something that may cause offense?

These questions are not just hypothetical. Caring people face such questions in relating to family and friends. Because we care, we tell them the truth as lovingly as we can, even if their response may cause us pain.

That is exactly what is at issue with Jewish evangelism. Our Jewish people do not want to hear the gospel; many think they know what we are going to say and have already decided it does not apply to them. The most loving thing we can do is to tell them, as carefully as possible, what Jesus has done for them. Yet many Christians are finding it difficult to believe that Jews really do need Jesus. Why?

The Jewish people have walked a long road of persecution. Sadly, Church history has been a major intersection on that road. Christians are becoming increasingly aware of that history, and of the fact that some who claimed to represent Jesus used His name to commit atrocities against the Jewish people. Many Christians are now deeply sensitized to anything that smacks of anti-Semitism. As Jews for Jesus, we are grateful for that sensitivity, especially when it leads people to be extra tactful and loving in sharing the gospel.

At the same time, some Christian friends have taken their
sensitivity in a different direction. They have concluded that
Jewish people do not need Jesus, and that it is unkind and
arrogant—even anti-Semitic—to suggest that they do. In many
cases, these conclusions are drawn from discussions with
Jewish friends whose opinions these Christians greatly value.
After all, when you respect and care for friends it is only
natural to take them at their word about such things,
especially when they speak with strong conviction.
And yet, Jesus also spoke with conviction when He
announced: "I am the way, the truth, and the life. No one
comes to the Father except through me" (John 14:6). We
believe that accepting Christ's claims means accepting the
privilege and the burden of communicating His claims to
others, even if they are insulted by the prospect.

The apostle Paul holds a key to the question of why we
continue reaching out to those who insist they do not need or
want the gospel. In Romans 11, he spoke of a partial hardening,
a spiritual blindness that has come to the people of Israel.

If the Bible is not God's truth for us, such talk about
blindness and hardening is demeaning. Certainly, if it were a
matter of Paul's personal opinion it would be. But if the Bible
is true, the reality is that Jewish people as a whole are
committed to disbelieving the gospel because they cannot, at
this point in history, see the truth. Paul says this "partial
blindness" is not complete, nor is it permanent. Most people
know that Jesus' first followers were Jewish, and that the first
Christian missionaries were "converted Jews" preaching the
gospel to Gentiles. Yet, in a sense, they were not converted
Jews—they were converted sinners who happened to be
Jewish. And they remained Jewish, never renouncing their
heritage or the faith of their ancestors. They were part of a
believing remnant of Jews whom God is calling to follow

Jesus. We Jews for Jesus are part of that believing remnant, and our efforts to make the gospel an unavoidable issue to the rest of our people are adding to that remnant.

As Jews who believe in Jesus, we sympathize with those who feel offended by the gospel, yet we do not accept the notion that it is offensive to tell Jewish people about Jesus. Many of us were offended the first time someone tried to share their faith with us. We know that there is some choice involved in being offended, and we also know that a negative reaction is not necessarily the end of the story—we have been there! We Jews who have found faith and everlasting life in Jesus recall how we once felt. Most of us considered anyone who confronted us with the gospel a minor annoyance at best, if not a major aggravation. Now we thank God for those who cared enough to tell us what we did not wish to hear. Can we do less than was done for us?

It's been said that most people are looking for God about as much as someone playing hooky is looking for a truant officer. That applies even more to Jewish people looking for Jesus! It's no wonder that our desire to make Him an unavoidable issue is considered intrusive by many. Yet our mission is not to intrude. It is simply to call attention to the Savior in ways that Jewish people cannot dismiss as being for someone else. We believe it is possible to draw attention to Jesus in respectful, loving and good natured ways. But it is always a battle to go against popular opinion, which tells us to keep the gospel to ourselves.

We are grateful for the many Christians who stand with us and are willing to face discomfort for the sake of Christ, and for their concern to see Jewish friends heavenbound. Still, the controversial nature of our cause makes it difficult for us to gain the friendship and support of many Christians who feel it's not quite polite to tell people who have their own religion that they need Jesus. We can only hope those Christians will think through the implications of that line of thinking. What if the Apostles Peter and Paul had decided it was impolite or disrespectful to tell Gentiles (who also had their own religions) about Jesus? There would be very few Christians in the world today!

It is not our task to buttonhole or force people to converse with us. Once we present people with an invitation to interact with our message—be it a gospel tract, a billboard, a gospel ad or even a phone call—they can choose to avoid, embrace, or seek further information about Jesus. If it's either of the latter two, we want to help.

HOW DOES THE JEWISH COMMUNITY RESPOND TO FORTHRIGHT EVANGELISM?

We have organized opposition which, oddly enough, encourages us. Our opposition points to the fact that more and more Jews are coming to faith in Jesus. We are honored to be "blamed," but God deserves the credit. We lift up Jesus, but He alone can draw Jews and Gentiles to Himself.

Rabbis and Jewish community leaders cannot allow themselves to believe that it is legitimate for a Jew to believe in Jesus, so many attempt to delegitimize us. Some allege that we are a cult or an exotic new religion, but most will say we are dishonest and disingenuous. (The latter accusations refer to our refusal to give up our Jewish identity as dishonest, since they believe that anyone who believes in Jesus cannot be Jewish.) In part, their attempts to undermine our credibility are meant to keep Jewish seekers away from us. However, our opposition also understands that we depend upon the friendship and support of our brothers and sisters in Christ. Statements undermining the integrity of Jewish evangelism drive a wedge between us and many members of Christ's Body.

HOW SUCCESSFUL IS THE OPPOSITION?

When it comes to keeping Jewish people from hearing us, our opposition mostly affects those who are not prepared to "go against the flow." Frankly, any Jewish people who would seriously consider Jesus are already questioning religious authorities and realizing they must investigate certain issues for themselves.

Ironically, our opposition seems to have more success within the Church. It has become increasingly popular among liberal and even among some not-so-liberal Christians to say that Jews have salvation apart from Christ. Therefore, they say that evangelizing Jewish people is an unnecessary, even unchristian, endeavor. *This is what happens when Christians view the Great Commission through the eyes of unbelieving friends and colleagues.*

Whereas empathy for the sensitivities of Jewish people is appreciated, it becomes tragic when allowed to take the place of a Bible-based philosophy of missions. How can one surmise from Scripture that it is insulting to speak to Jews of the love of Jesus, who came as a Jew? How can it be insulting to tell of the great sacrifice He made for all people? How can it be insulting to offer the abundant life He gives?

Unbelieving Jewish people who are willing to go against the flow to explore the gospel have a sense of what is at stake—their own salvation. Unfortunately, too many Christians do not have that urgent sense of what is at stake. For some, the friendship or respect of unsaved Jewish people seems to determine their view of Jewish evangelism. Saying that Jesus is the only way to salvation would mean risking rejection. As Jews who are for Jesus, we have no choice but to make that statement and take the heat. If we were not convinced that Jesus is the only way of salvation, we would not have given up the respect and acceptance of the

Jewish community. Since we are convinced that the salvation of our people is at stake, we *have* to reach out and take the risk.

Appendix F
The Willowbank Declaration

"The Gospel is the power of God for salvation, to everyone who believes, to the Jew first and also to the Greek." (Romans 1:16)

"Brethren, my heart's desire and prayer to God for Israel is that they may be saved." (Romans 10:1)

THE WILLOWBANK DECLARATION ON THE CHRISTIAN GOSPEL AND THE JEWISH PEOPLE

PREAMBLE

Every Christian must acknowledge an immense debt of gratitude to the Jewish people. The Gospel is the good news that Jesus is the Christ, the long-promised Jewish Messiah, who by his life, death and resurrection saves from sin and all its consequences. Those who worship Jesus as their Divine Lord and Saviour have thus received God's most precious gift through the Jewish people. Therefore they have compelling reason to show love to that people in every possible way.

Concerned about humanity everywhere, we are resolved to uphold the right of Jewish people to a just and peaceful existence everywhere, both in the land of Israel and in their communities throughout the world. We repudiate past persecutions of Jews by those identified as Christians, and we pledge ourselves to resist every form of anti-Semitism. As the supreme way of demonstrating love, we seek to encourage the Jewish people, along with all other peoples, to receive God's gift of life through Jesus the Messiah, and accordingly the growing number of Jewish Christians brings us great joy.

In making this Declaration we stand in a long and revered Christian tradition, which in 1980 was highlighted by a landmark statement, "Christian Witness to the Jewish People," issued by the Lausanne Committee for World Evangelization. Now, at this Willowbank Consultation on the Gospel and the Jewish People, sponsored by the World Evangelical Fellowship and supported by the Lausanne Committee, we reaffirm our commitment to the Jewish people and our desire to share the Gospel with them.

This Declaration is made in response to growing doubts and widespread confusion among Christians about the need for, and the propriety of, endeavors to share faith in Jesus Christ with Jewish people. Several factors unite to produce the uncertain state of mind that the Declaration seeks to resolve.

The Holocaust, perpetrated as it was by leaders and citizens of a supposedly Christian nation, has led to a sense in some quarters that Christian credibility among Jews has been totally destroyed. Accordingly, some have shrunk back from addressing the Jewish people with the Gospel.

Some who see the creation of the state of Israel as a direct fulfillment of biblical prophecy have concluded that the Christian task at this time is to "comfort Israel" by supporting this new political entity, rather than to challenge Jews by direct evangelism.

Some church leaders have retreated from embracing the task of evangelizing Jews as a responsibility of Christian mission. Rather, a new theology is being embraced which holds that God's covenant with Israel through Abraham establishes all Jews in God's favor for all times, and so makes faith in Jesus Christ for salvation needless so far as they are concerned.

On this basis, it is argued that dialogue with Jews in order to understand each other better, and cooperation in the quest for socio-economic shalom, is all that Christian mission requires in relation to the Jewish people. Continued attempts to do what the Church has done from the first, in seeking to win Jews to Jesus as Messiah, are widely opposed and decried, by Christian as well as Jewish leaders.

Attempts to bring Jews to faith in Jesus are frequently denounced as proselytizing. This term is often used to imply dishonest and coercive modes of inducement, appeal to unworthy motives, and disregard of the question of truth even though it is truth that is being disseminated. In recent years, "Messianic" Jewish believers in Jesus, who as Christians celebrate and maximize their Jewish identity, have emerged as active evangelists to the Jewish community. Jewish leaders often accused them of deception on the grounds that one cannot be both a Jew and a Christian. While these criticisms may reflect Judaism's current effort to define itself as a distinct religion in opposition to Christianity, they have led to much bewilderment and some misunderstanding and mistrust.

The Declaration responds to this complex situation and seeks to set directions for the future according to the Scriptures.

I. THE DEMAND OF THE GOSPEL
Article I.1
WE AFFIRM THAT the redeeming love of God has been fully and finally revealed in Jesus Christ.

WE DENY THAT those without faith in Christ know the full reality of God's love and of the gift that he gives.

Article I.2
WE AFFIRM THAT the God-given types, prophecies and visions of

salvation and shalom in the Hebrew Scriptures find their present and future fulfillment in and through Jesus Christ, the Son of God, who by incarnation became a Jew and was shown to be the Son of God and Messiah by his resurrection.

WE DENY THAT it is right to look for a Messiah who has not yet appeared in world history.

Article I.3
WE AFFIRM THAT Jesus Christ is the second person of the one God, who became a man, lived a perfect life, shed his blood on the cross as an atoning sacrifice for human sins, rose bodily from the dead, now reigns as Lord, and will return visibly to this earth, all to fulfill the purpose of bringing sinners to share eternally in his fellowship and glory.

WE DENY THAT those who think of Jesus Christ in lesser terms than these have faith in him in any adequate sense.

Article I.4
WE AFFIRM THAT all human beings are sinful by nature and practice, and stand condemned, helpless and hopeless, before God, until the grace of Christ touches their lives and brings them to God's pardon and peace.

WE DENY THAT any Jew or Gentile finds true peace with God through performing works of law.

Article I.5
WE AFFIRM THAT God's forgiveness of the penitent rests on the satisfaction rendered to his justice by the substitutionary sacrifice of Jesus Christ on the cross.

WE DENY THAT any person can enjoy God's favor apart from the mediation of Jesus Christ, the sin-bearer.

Article I.6

WE AFFIRM THAT those who turn to Jesus Christ find him to be a
sufficient Saviour and Deliverer from all the evil of sin: from its
guilt, shame, power, and perversity; from blind defiance of God,
debasement of moral character, and the dehumanizing and
destructive self-assertion that sin breeds.

WE DENY THAT the salvation found in Christ may be
supplemented in any way.

Article I.7

WE AFFIRM THAT faith in Jesus Christ is humanity's only way
to come to know the Creator as Father, according to Christ's
own Word: "I am the Way and the Truth and the Life; no one
comes to the Father except through me" (John 14:6).

WE DENY THAT any non-Christian faith, as such, will mediate
eternal life with God.

II. THE CHURCH OF JEWS AND GENTILES
Article II.8

WE AFFIRM THAT through the mediation of Jesus Christ, God has
made a new covenant with Jewish and Gentile believers,
pardoning their sins, writing his law on their hearts by his Spirit,
so that they obey him, giving the Holy Spirit to indwell them, and
bringing each one to know him by faith in a relationship of
trustful gratitude for salvation.

WE DENY THAT the blessings of the New Covenant belong to
any except believers in Jesus Christ.

Article II.9

WE AFFIRM THAT the profession of continuing Jewish identity, for
which Hebrew Christians have in the past suffered at the hands of

both their fellow-Jews and Gentile church leaders, was consistent with the Christian Scriptures and with the nature of the church as one body in Jesus Christ in which Jews and non-Jews are united. WE DENY THAT it is necessary for Jewish Christians to repudiate their Jewish heritage.

Article II.10
WE AFFIRM THAT Gentile believers, who at present constitute the great bulk of the Christian church, are included in the historically continuous community of believing people on earth which Paul pictures as God's olive tree (Romans 11:13-24).

WE DENY THAT Christian faith is necessarily non-Jewish, and that Gentiles who believe in Christ may ignore their solidarity with believing Jews, or formulate their new identity in Christ without reference to Jewishness, or decline to receive the Hebrew Scriptures as part of their own instruction from God, or refuse to see themselves as having their roots in Jewish history.

Article II.11
WE AFFIRM THAT Jewish people who come to faith in Messiah have liberty before God to observe or not observe traditional Jewish customs and ceremonies that are consistent with the Christian Scriptures and do not hinder fellowship with the rest of the Body of Christ.

WE DENY THAT any inconsistency or deception is involved by Jewish Christians representing themselves as "Messianic" or "completed" or "fulfilled" Jews.

III. GOD'S PLAN FOR THE JEWISH PEOPLE
Article III.12
WE AFFIRM THAT Jewish people have an ongoing part in God's plan.

WE DENY THAT indifference to the future of the Jewish people on the part of Christians can ever be justified.

Article III.13
WE AFFIRM THAT prior to the coming of Christ it was Israel's unique privilege to enjoy a corporate covenantal relationship with God, following upon the national redemption from slavery, and involving God's gift of the law and of a theocratic culture; God's promise of blessing to faithful obedience; and God's provision of atonement for transgression.

WE AFFIRM THAT within this covenant relationship, God's pardon and acceptance of the penitent which was linked to the offering of prescribed sacrifices rested upon the fore-ordained sacrifice of Jesus Christ.

WE DENY THAT covenantal privilege alone can ever bring salvation to impenitent unbelievers.

Article III.14
WE AFFIRM THAT much of Judaism, in its various forms, throughout contemporary Israel and today's Diaspora, is a development out of, rather than as an authentic embodiment of, the faith, love and hope that the Hebrew Scriptures teach.

WE DENY THAT modern Judaism with its explicit negation of the divine person, work, and Messiahship of Jesus Christ contains within itself true knowledge of God's salvation.

Article III.15
WE AFFIRM THAT the biblical hope for Jewish people centers on their being restored through faith in Christ to their proper place as branches of God's olive tree from which they are at present broken off.

WE DENY THAT the historical status of the Jews as God's people brings salvation to any Jew who does not accept the claims of Jesus Christ.

Article III.16
WE AFFIRM THAT the Bible promises that large numbers of Jews will turn to Christ through God's sovereign grace.

WE DENY THAT this prospect renders needless the active proclamation of the gospel to Jewish people in this and every age.

Article III.17
WE AFFIRM THAT anti-Semitism on the part of professed Christians has always been wicked and shameful and that the church has in the past been much to blame for tolerating and encouraging it and for condoning anti-Jewish actions on the part of individuals and governments.

WE DENY THAT these past failures, for which offending Gentile believers must ask forgiveness from both God and the Jewish community, rob Christians of the right or lessen their responsibility to share the Gospel with Jews today and for the future.

Article III.18
WE AFFIRM THAT it was the sins of the whole human race that sent Christ to the cross.

WE DENY THAT it is right to single out the Jewish people for putting Jesus to death.

IV. EVANGELISM AND THE JEWISH PEOPLE
Article IV.19
WE AFFIRM THAT sharing the Good News of Jesus Christ

with lost humanity is a matter of prime obligation for Christian people, both because the Messiah commands the making of disciples and because love of neighbor requires effort to meet our neighbor's deepest need.

WE DENY THAT any other form of witness and service to others can excuse Christians from laboring to bring them to faith in Christ.

Article IV.20
WE AFFIRM THAT the church's obligation to share saving knowledge of Christ with the whole human race includes the evangelizing of Jewish people as a priority: "To the Jew first" (Romans 1:16).

WE DENY THAT dialogue with Jewish people that aims at nothing more than mutual understanding constitutes fulfillment of this obligation.

Article IV.21
WE AFFIRM THAT the concern to point Jewish people to faith in Jesus Christ which the Christian church has historically felt and shown was right.

WE DENY THAT there is any truth in the widespread notion that evangelizing Jews is needless because they are already in covenant with God through Abraham and Moses and so are already saved despite their rejection of Jesus Christ as Lord and Saviour.

Article IV.22
WE AFFIRM THAT all endeavours to persuade others to become Christians should express love to them by respecting their dignity and integrity at every point, including parents' responsibility in the case of their children.

WE DENY THAT coercive or deceptive proselytizing, which violates dignity and integrity on both sides, can ever be justified.

Article IV.23
WE AFFIRM THAT it is unchristian, unloving, and discriminatory to propose a moratorium on the evangelizing of any part of the human race, and that failure to preach the gospel to the Jewish people would be a form of anti-Semitism, depriving this particular community of its right to hear the gospel.

WE DENY THAT we have sufficient warrant to assume or anticipate the salvation of anyone who is not a believer in Jesus Christ.

Article IV.24
WE AFFIRM THAT the existence of separate churchly organizations for evangelizing Jews, as for evangelizing any other particular human group, can be justified pragmatically, as an appropriate means of fulfilling the church's mandate to take the Gospel to the whole human race.

WE DENY THAT the depth of human spiritual need varies from group to group so that Jewish people may be thought to need Christ either more or less than others.

V. JEWISH-CHRISTIAN RELATIONS
Article V.25
WE AFFIRM THAT dialogue with other faiths that seeks to transcend stereotypes of them based on ignorance, and to find common ground and to share common concerns, is an expression of Christian love that should be encouraged.

WE DENY THAT dialogue that explains the Christian faith without seeking to persuade the dialogue partners of its truth and claims is a sufficient expression of Christian love.

Article V.26
WE AFFIRM THAT for Christians and non-Christian Jews to make common cause in social witness and action, contending together for freedom of speech and religion, the value of the individual, and the moral standards of God's law is right and good.

WE DENY THAT such limited cooperation involves any compromise of the distinctive views of either community or imposes any restraint upon Christians in seeking to share the Gospel with the Jews with whom they cooperate.

Article V.27
WE AFFIRM THAT the Jewish quest for a homeland with secure borders and a just peace has our support.

WE DENY THAT any biblical link between the Jewish people and the land of Israel justifies actions that contradict biblical ethics and constitute oppression of people-groups or individuals.

SPONSOR: WORLD EVANGELICAL FELLOWSHIP
INTERNATIONAL HEADQUARTERS
1, Sophia Road #07-09
Peace Centre
SINGAPORE 0922

WEF North American Headquarters
P. O. Box WEF
Wheaton, IL 60189

This Declaration was developed and adopted on April 29, 1989 by all those present at the Consultation on the Gospel and the Jewish People after several days of intense consultation, undergirded by prayer. Together the participants commend this document to the churches with a call to prayerfully consider and act upon these very serious matters as touching the Christian Gospel and the Jewish People.

Dr. Vernon Grounds (Chairman) U.S.A.; Dr. Tokunboh Adeyemo, KENYA; Dr. Henri Blocher, FRANCE; Dr. Tormod Engelsviken, NORWAY; Dr. Arthur Glasser, U.S.A.; Dr. Robert Godfrey, U.S.A.; Mrs. Gretchen Gaebelein Hull, U.S.A.; Dr. Kenneth Kantzer, U.S.A.; Rev. Ole Chr. Kvarme, NORWAY; Dr. David Lim, PHILIPPINES; Rev. Murdo MacLeod, ENGLAND; Dr. J. I. Packer, CANADA; Dr. Bong Ro R.O.C.; Dr. Sunand Sumithra, INDIA; Dr. David Wells, U.S.A.; Tuvya Zaretsky, U.S.A.

Appendix G
A Final Word from David Brickner, Executive Director of Jews for Jesus

AN OPEN LETTER TO THE FAMILY OF JEWISH BELIEVERS IN JESUS

In the first century, Jewish believers in Jesus were the Church's leaders, worldwide. The apostles and those they mentored set an example for this far-flung and diverse community of faith. They provided instruction, primarily in letter form. Those "epistles" that were uniquely inspired by the Holy Spirit became sacred Scripture. One such epistle, Hebrews, addressed perplexing matters of crucial concern primarily to first-century Jewish believers.

Many Jewish followers of Jesus face the same crucial concerns today. This open letter to Jewish followers of Jesus directs us back to the wisdom of the book of Hebrews and seven challenges to my Messianic family:

1. Love Y'shua
2. Love His Body
3. Resist the lure of triumphalism
4. Resist the lure of rabbinic Judaism
5. Resist the lure of assimilation
6. Proclaim the gospel
7. Proclaim the return of Messiah

We live in a world of deafening noises and competing demands for our attention and our affections. When the world shouts out obvious temptations to ungodliness we have a clear choice to avoid sin or fall prey to it. The choice is not always so clear when urgent and earnest voices tempt us in high-minded and spiritual-sounding terminology. The way to recognize these other temptations is the same as it was in the first century: fall deeply in love with Jesus. *Veyahaftah et Adonai Y'shua elohecha, vechol levavcha.* (And you shall love the Lord Jesus your God with all your heart.)

The author of Hebrews spent considerable time emphasizing the glories of Messiah Jesus. Jewish believers understood the dangers of idolatry, but many were confused concerning the very proper and biblical adoration of the God/man, Y'shua HaMashiach. Accordingly, the first three verses of the book of Hebrews present a beautiful clarification of Christ's deity.

> God, who at various times and in various ways spoke in time past to the fathers by the prophets, has in these last days spoken to us by His Son, (1) whom He has appointed heir of all things, (2) through whom also He made the worlds; (3) who being the brightness of His glory (4) and the express image of His person, and (5) upholding all things by the word of His power, (6) when He had by Himself purged our sins, (7) sat down at the right hand of the Majesty on high. (Hebrews 1:1-3)

Using a rabbinical device known as "stringing pearls," the author of Hebrews proclaims a seven-fold majesty of Messiah Jesus (indicated by the numbers in parentheses that I have inserted into the text). Y'shua's deity is never in question. His glory is equal to that of the Father.

As Jewish believers, we should be leading the exaltation of our Messiah Jesus. Yet certain claims seen in the above passage are de-emphasized among some (repeat, *some*) of the Messianic brothers and sisters. Of course, this would make sense if traditional Judaism were our model—since it is not traditional for Jews to believe in Jesus and the rabbis insist that believers in Him are no longer Jewish. If the rabbis were right and we could not be Jewish and believe what the New Testament says about Jesus, I hope we would be willing to choose our Jesus over our Jewish identity.

Fortunately, the rabbis are absolutely wrong. The most Jewish thing any of us could do is believe in and lovingly follow Jesus our Messiah. We need to express our love for Jesus in ways that are both theologically rich and devotionally warmhearted. Our "Jesusness" is more important than our Jewishness— because we can be reconciled to God whether or not we are Jewish, whereas we cannot be reconciled to Him without faith in Jesus. And our destiny as human beings rests on whether or not we are reconciled to God. That is not to trivialize our Jewish identity, which is a precious gift from God. But the gift cannot be elevated above the Giver.

Our love for Jesus will also help us to love one another more fully. I don't know if there has been a time in recent history when Jewish believers in Jesus have been more divided from one another than we are at present. A host of issues seems to come between us. But if we truly love Jesus with our whole hearts, we will love one another as He loves us. Our differences and disputes will pale in the light of our passionate adoration for the Messiah, who truly makes us one in Him.

Indeed, if we fall in love again with Jesus, we will more fully love His Body (the Church) in all of its diversity. Y'shua's love for the Church is described as the love of a husband for his wife: "Husbands, love your wives, *just as Christ also loved the church* and gave Himself for her" (Ephesians 5:25). How can anyone fully love Messiah without having a proper appreciation for His beloved Church?

We are all very sensitive to the terror and tragedy of past Christian anti-Semitism, particularly in Europe. This has been a

stain on the reputation of Christianity—a mark that we
Messianic Jews do not wish to bear. Some Jewish believers
draw away from the Church to avoid guilt-by-association—
even though the majority of the Church (which includes all of
Jesus' disciples to this day) had no part in that guilt. Ironically,
the majority of Jesus-followers in the world today are from
African, Latin and Asian parts of the world. Neither they nor
their ancestors had any part in the terrible chapters of church-
related anti-Semitism. Our unbelieving Jewish people may
paint the Church with a broad stroke of the brush, but we
who know Jesus and know His people have no business
laying responsibility for anti-Semitism at the feet of those who
had nothing to do with it. If we allow the past to control our
present attitude toward the Church, we will be guilty of
holding in contempt what God loves.

When the God of Israel looks on His Church today, He sees a
colorful mosaic of people from every tribe and tongue and
nation. We Jewish believers have an important part in that
mosaic. There has been an emphasis on recovering the Jewish
roots of faith in Jesus and I applaud this. But we must beware
of "cultural imperialism." Christians are enriched through
understanding the Jewish backgrounds of the Christian faith,
but we cannot reincarnate today's Church to be a first century
Jewish expression of faith in Christ. We should not berate our
non-Jewish brethren for their own cultural expressions of faith
in Christ as though it were some kind of paganism.

Despite the problems of history, God's people have been
exceedingly good to us Jewish believers in Jesus. They have loved
us. They have welcomed us as family when our own families
rejected us for our faith in Messiah. They have been patient with
our immaturities. They have encouraged our attempts to express
our Jewish identity alongside our faith in Christ. They have
generously supported our efforts to make Messiah known among
our own people. We cannot ask for much more than that.

God never intended the Church to be entirely Jewish. He established a richness of cultural diversity in the worship of Israel's Messiah for all time and eternity. Let us celebrate that diversity and humbly take guidance from the future vision of John the Apostle: "After these things I looked, and behold, a great multitude which no one could number, of all nations, tribes, peoples, and tongues, standing before the throne and before the Lamb, clothed with white robes, with palm branches in their hands, and crying out with a loud voice, saying, 'Salvation belongs to our God who sits on the throne, and to the Lamb!'" (Revelation 7:9-10).

If we as Jewish believers want to be as we were in the first century, an example to the rest of the Church, let it begin with two emphases. Let us love Messiah Jesus completely and passionately and let us love His Body, the Church, fully and without reservation.

RESIST THE LURE OF TRIUMPHALISM
When Jewish people become followers of Jesus we face several problems. Most commonly, there is stress and in some cases estrangement from unbelieving family members. But there are other problems that are far less obvious. For example, there's the pedestal problem: the new Jewish believer is immediately given a place of prominence in the local church simply because he or she happens to have been born Jewish. Suddenly, this baby believer is sought out as an expert in the Old Testament. Many well-meaning Christians mistakenly think that all Jews are thoroughly conversant with the Hebrew Bible. Most Jewish believers know that this is not the case and many are keenly aware of their own lack of biblical knowledge. Yet it can be very embarrassing to admit that lack. It can also be difficult for a new and spiritually immature believer to resist the flattery of Christian friends. Some of us have been tempted to think higher of ourselves

than we ought to, despite the clear admonition of the Scriptures (Romans 12:3).

This danger applies not only to new Jewish believers, but also to some that have been in the faith long enough to know better. God has placed a special love for Jewish people in the hearts of many Christians and, as a result, we Messianic Jews are at times treated to a place of honor in the Body of Christ. Some have begun to believe that we actually deserve it. In fact, there are those who are calling for the restoration of Jewish believers to a place of leadership over the Church, just as it was in the first century. This is wrongheaded triumphalism and some Christians have added their endorsement to it.

God has been doing something wonderful in bringing greater numbers of Jewish people to Jesus in modern times, and the Church should give glory to God by acknowledging and affirming this work of grace. However, the Church needs leaders who, by piety and strength of godly conviction, show the way forward for the rest of Christ's followers. Whether one is Jewish or Gentile has no bearing on that piety and godly conviction.

Ours is a small and relatively immature movement within the Body of Christ, one that has not yet led the way in growth or unity. And while some in our ranks are unusually bright and gifted, as a whole we are not particularly exemplary in scholarship or sanctification. The fact is, we haven't been doing such a good job leading ourselves, let alone anyone else. And though I'm embarrassed to admit it, there may be a subtle racism in the notion that Jewish believers should be given prominence within the Body of Christ.

Unless or until we Messianic Jews are qualified to lead, we should not expect or accept leadership or prominence in the

Church—and we certainly should not seek it on the basis of our ethnicity or even historic precedent (Proverbs 27:2).

RESIST THE LURE OF RABBINIC JUDAISM

The demographics of the Messianic movement reflect those of the wider Jewish community, which means most were raised in fairly secular Jewish homes. Many Jewish believers learn more about what it means to be Jewish after coming to faith in Jesus—which leads to an altogether appropriate appreciation for their Jewish heritage. However, some want to make up for lost time by becoming "more Jewish," and that is when Jewish believers become vulnerable to a different kind of temptation.

The mature Jewish believer recognizes that Jewish religious leaders, particularly rabbis, are going to deny our identity as Jews unless we deny certain things about Jesus, or agree to keep silent about them. That recognition serves as a warning not to seek their affirmation because it comes at a cost we can't pay. Yet some in our Messianic movement remain uncertain about the relationship of Jewish believers to rabbinic Judaism.

It is understandable that Jewish believers want to be "authentically" Jewish while still following Jesus. But what does that actually mean? Who is to say what it means to be authentic in one's Jewish identity? The rabbis have pronounced themselves the trustees and guardians of what is authentically Jewish. It stands to reason that anyone who is working out his or her Jewish identity will be drawn to rabbinic teaching. Some of the teaching and tradition is good and wise. However, the rabbis are inherently opposed to our faith in Jesus and hostile to our desire to tell other Jews about Him. Do we really want to look to their standards to validate whether or not we are authentically Jewish?

Validation can be a big problem for Jewish believers. Where do we look for it? It is easy to fall prey to our own pride and desire for acceptance from our fellow Jews—and often we don't see those things for what they are. Pride is especially hard to pinpoint when it is hiding behind more noble qualities such as piety or zeal for God.

Some Messianic Jews are teaching that it is incumbent on all Jewish believers to observe the Law of Moses and to worship exclusively in Messianic congregations. They would agree that we are saved by grace through faith in Messiah Jesus. However, they would add that Jewish believers who want to fulfill their destiny as Messianic Jews must continue to be a part of the Jewish community, which means living a "Torah-observant" lifestyle, a lifestyle that can only really be lived out in the context of a community of Messianic Jews. I have heard of instances where, failing to find a Messianic congregation in the area, some Jewish believers have chosen to attend a synagogue rather than a church. This is a form of neo-Galatianism, pure and simple (Galatians 3:2-3).

There is nothing wrong with celebrating the biblical feasts or following certain rabbinical traditions, but we can do so only to the extent that we do not contradict the clear teaching of the Scriptures, both Old and New Testaments. And part of that New Testament teaching is that, in Messiah, we are fully free to practice these things or not as a matter of choice and conscience.

To declare rabbinical teachings and traditions obligatory in any way for the follower of Jesus, or to seek acceptance as Jews at the expense of our forthright identification with Christ, puts us on a slippery slope towards spiritual disaster. It has caused many people to separate from brothers and sisters in the Church, and eventually from Christ Himself.

The Messianic Jews of the first century faced similar temptations under more dire circumstances. They were subject to Roman prosecution for refusing to pay homage to Caesar. They had only to return to the synagogue to be granted immunity for not participating in this forced idolatry. However, they would only be accepted in the synagogue if they did not speak of their faith in Jesus.

The author of Hebrews admonished them: "Therefore Jesus also, that He might sanctify the people with His own blood, suffered outside the gate. Therefore let us go forth to Him, outside the camp, bearing His reproach" (Hebrews 13:12-13).

To bear the reproach of the Messiah is a badge of honor, not of shame. Are we willing to bear that reproach, even if it means going "outside the camp" of what the rabbis consider authentically Jewish?

Jesus is our rabbi as well as our Savior and Lord. He freely interacted with the teaching of the rabbis. Where He was in agreement with them, He said so. But when He was at odds with the rabbis, He clearly spoke out. The crowds recognized that Jesus taught with authority and not as the scribes (the rabbis) of the first century (Matthew 7:29). Shouldn't those of us who claim Jesus as our authority give Him the honor and obedience He so rightly deserves?

RESIST THE LURE OF ASSIMILATION
"Why don't you just call yourself a Christian?" I can't count the number of times I have been asked this "question," which often sounds more like an accusation.

When it comes from unbelieving Jewish people, I take it to mean, "If you want to believe in Jesus that is your business. But calling yourself a Jew makes it my business. Just call

yourself a Christian so I can go on believing that Jesus is not
for Jews and therefore not for me."

When Christians ask the question, it usually indicates a
misunderstanding about our Jewish identity. Is it a matter of
ethnic pride, and an effort to disassociate from the rest of the
Body of Christ? Is it a desire to return to works salvation?

The easiest thing *would* be to "just call ourselves Christians,"
(identify *only* as Christians and forsake our Jewish identity). Many
Jewish believers in Jesus have chosen to do just that. But the
trend to assimilate, or to blend into the larger culture, is not
unique to those Jewish believers. Many Jews who don't believe in
Jesus have chosen to walk away from their Jewish identity, making
assimilation a top concern among Jewish leaders worldwide.

Nevertheless, the lure to assimilate can be even more powerful
for Jewish believers in Jesus. The Jewish community insists
that it is deceptive for us to call ourselves Jews, and many in
the Christian community appear confused or even hurt when
we maintain our identity. Caught between the two, many
Jewish believers in Jesus feel uncertain about how Jewishness
and Jesus go together. Assimilation beckons with the promise
to end the uncertainty and the accompanying angst.

I want to challenge Jewish believers to resist that lure. We
need to remember that God still has a plan for the Jewish
people. "God has not cast away His people whom He
foreknew" (Romans 11:2a). The first and most compelling
evidence of that ongoing plan is the presence of Jewish
believers in Jesus: "Even so then, at this present time there is a
remnant according to the election of grace" (Romans 11:5).

Identifying as a Jew is not a rejection of God's grace. Rather,
that remnant of Jewish believers stands as a testimony to

God's grace. Moreover, there is no such thing as an invisible remnant or an undetectable testimony.

The Apostle Paul believed that his Jewish identity was evidence of God's gracious choice. Ethnic pride or a "middle wall of partition" had nothing to do with it, nor should it for us. None of us can claim any credit for having been born Jewish—we had no choice in the matter. God made us that way and the Scriptures teach us: "Let each one remain in the same calling in which he was called" (1 Corinthians 7:20).

Each individual must work out what that means and how they choose to remain a visible part of this remnant. For many, their Jewish identity will remain similar to what it was before they received Christ. That might mean a mostly cultural expression—with little felt need to express Jewishness through special observances. Other people prefer a more active approach to Jewish identity, such as Shabbat dinners, festival celebrations or participation in a Messianic fellowship or congregation. These choices are especially important when it comes to succeeding generations. However, by maintaining our Jewish identity in some form or other, we bear witness to the grace of God and His continuing purposes for the Jewish people.

PROCLAIM THE GOSPEL AND THE RETURN OF MESSIAH

Which brings me to this: Our calling as Jews is never more fulfilled than when we are proclaiming the good news of Messiah Jesus. My colleague Avi Snyder has pointed out that our people were created to proclaim. We were chosen to be a "light to the nations," and that is not a passive role.

Ultimately, God fulfilled His far-reaching intention through Israel's greater Son, the Messiah Jesus. Through His blood He purchased our salvation and the salvation of all who trust in Him. That is why Jewish believers in Jesus are never more fulfilled in our destiny than when we are fully engaged in proclaiming His Messiahship and His salvation. It is His light and His message that can give hope to a lost and dying world. Yet many Jewish believers when challenged to proclaim the gospel (especially to our fellow Jews), behave like Jonah when God called him to Nineveh—and there are many ships headed to Tarshish. What kind of giant fish will it take to turn us toward our true destiny?

It need not be a crisis—a renewed confidence in Messiah's return can also help us on our way. And that is my final point. We need to believe and actively proclaim that the coming of the Lord draws near.

The belief that Y'shua (Jesus) could return at any moment is not wishful thinking. It is our "blessed hope" (Titus 2:13). God intends that hope to compel us to holy, unashamed and unreserved gospel proclamation. The risen Lord of glory might step through the portals of heaven at any moment! This should be at the forefront of our minds and hearts, motivating us to be a light to the nations, now and until He comes again.

James, the leader of the Messianic movement in Jerusalem, admonished the remnant of Jewish believers under his care, "You also be patient. Establish your hearts, for the coming of the Lord is at hand" (James 5:8). The author of Hebrews encouraged those early Jewish believers to continue in active fellowship, ". . . exhorting one another, and so much the more as you see the Day approaching" (Hebrews 10:25). Along with this we must remember with confidence the promises of God concerning His future purpose for our "countrymen according to the flesh" (Romans 9:3).

I am persuaded that as Jewish believers bear witness to our faith among our own people, we are sowing seeds for a harvest that is yet to come. In the same way that those first century Messianic Jews set the pace for the rest of the Body of Christ, so we Jewish believers in Jesus today ought to be an example of faith and hope in the soon coming of our Lord.

We share a glorious destiny with our brothers and sisters in Christ from every tribe and tongue and nation. That destiny is most beautifully depicted in the architecture of the New Jerusalem, bearing the names of the 12 tribes of Israel on its gates and the 12 apostles on its foundations (Revelation 21:12,14). God's people will ultimately be joined together in Messiah for all time and eternity. What a glorious future we have. Let's embrace that future here and now.